THE ACADEMIC PROFESSION

A SPECIAL REPORT

The Academic Profession

AN INTERNATIONAL PERSPECTIVE

ERNEST L. BOYER
PHILIP G. ALTBACH
MARY JEAN WHITELAW

THE CARNEGIE FOUNDATION
FOR THE ADVANCEMENT OF TEACHING

5 IVY LANE, PRINCETON, NEW JERSEY 08540

Copyright © 1994

The Carnegie Foundation
for the Advancement of Teaching

This report is published as part of the effort by The Carnegie Foundation for the Advancement of Teaching to explore significant issues in education. The views expressed should not necessarily be ascribed to individual members of the Board of Trustees of The Carnegie Foundation.

Copyright under International, Pan-American, and Universal Copyright Conventions. All rights reserved. No part of this book may be reproduced in any form—except for brief quotations not to exceed one thousand words in a review or professional work—without permission in writing from the publisher.

LIBRARY OF CONGRESS CATALOGING-IN-PUBLICATION DATA

Boyer, Ernest L.
    The academic profession : an international perspective / Ernest L. Boyer, Philip G. Altbach, Mary Jean Whitelaw.
        p.   cm. — (A Special report)
    Includes bibliographical references.
    ISBN 0-931050-47-2 : $8.00
        1. College teaching—Statistics. 2. College teachers—Employment—Statistics. 3. Comparative education. 4. Educational surveys.
I. Altbach, Philip G. II. Whitelaw, Mary Jean, 1957-
III. Carnegie Foundation for the Advancement of Teaching.
IV. Title. V. Series: Special report (Carnegie Foundation for the Advancement of Teaching)
LB2331.B62   1994
378.1′25′021 dc20   94-40363
                                                                           CIP

Copies are available from

CALIFORNIA/PRINCETON FULFILLMENT SERVICES
1445 Lower Ferry Road
Ewing, New Jersey 08618

TOLL-FREE—U.S. & CANADA (800) 777-4726   FAX (800) 999-1958

PHONE (609) 883-1759   FAX (609) 883-7413

CONTENTS

LIST OF FIGURES	vii	
LIST OF TABLES	xi	
ACKNOWLEDGMENTS	xv	
INTRODUCTION	*The International Professoriate: An Overview*	1
CHAPTER I	*Profile of the Professoriate*	5
CHAPTER II	*Students: Access and Excellence*	7
CHAPTER III	*Professional Activity: Teaching, Research, and Service*	11
CHAPTER IV	*Working Conditions: Satisfactions and Frustrations*	13
CHAPTER V	*Governing the Academy*	15
CHAPTER VI	*Higher Education and Society*	17
CHAPTER VII	*The International Dimension*	19
CHAPTER VIII	*Reflections: Prospects for the Future*	21
TECHNICAL NOTES	25	
APPENDIX	29	
FIGURES	33	
TABLES	71	

LIST OF FIGURES

FIGURE 1 What is your gender? 35

FIGURE 2 How old are you? 35

FIGURE 3 At how many different institutions of higher education have you ever held a regular academic appointment? 36

FIGURE 4 Is your current employment at this institution full time or part time? 36

FIGURE 5 Do you currently hold other paid academic positions outside this institution? 37

FIGURE 6 Do you currently hold other paid nonacademic positions outside this institution? 37

FIGURE 7 Of your total earned income, what percentage comes from this institution? 38

FIGURE 8 In your opinion, what percentage of the young people in your country are capable of completing secondary education? 38

FIGURE 9 In your opinion, what percentage of students in your country who complete secondary education should be admitted to higher eduction? 39

FIGURE 10 Access to higher education should be available to all who meet minimum entrance requirements. 39

FIGURE 11 Admission standards should be lowered to permit disadvantaged students to enroll at this institution. 40

FIGURE 12 The undergraduates you teach at this institution are adequately prepared in written and oral communication skills. 40

FIGURE 13 The undergraduates you teach at this institution are adequately prepared in mathematics and quantitative reasoning skills. 41

FIGURE 14 How would you rate the quality of the students currently enrolled in your department? 41

FIGURE 15 Please indicate the degree to which your affiliation with your academic discipline is important to you.   42

FIGURE 16 Please indicate the degree to which your affiliation with this institution is important to you.   42

FIGURE 17 Regarding your own preferences, do your interests lie primarily in teaching or in research?   43

FIGURE 18 The pressure to publish reduces the quality of teaching at this institution.   43

FIGURE 19 Have you or your research group received any grants or special funding in the last three years?   44

FIGURE 20 Please estimate the total amount of research funding you or your research group received in the last three years.   44

FIGURE 21 Research funding in my field is easier to get now than it was five years ago.   45

FIGURE 22 A strong record of successful research activity is important in faculty evaluation at this institution.   45

FIGURE 23 In my department, it is difficult for a person to achieve tenure if he or she does not publish.   46

FIGURE 24 I frequently feel under pressure to do more research than I actually would like to do.   46

FIGURE 25 Is your teaching regularly evaluated?   47

FIGURE 26 Is your research regularly evaluated?   47

FIGURE 27 Are your service activities regularly evaluated?   48

FIGURE 28 Student opinions should be used in evaluating the teaching effectiveness of faculty.   48

FIGURE 29 Is your teaching regularly evaluated by your students?   49

FIGURE 30 At this institution, we need better ways to evaluate teaching performance.   49

FIGURE 31 At this institution, publications used for promotion decisions are just "counted," not qualitatively evaluated.   50

FIGURE 32 How would you rate your own academic salary?   50

FIGURE 33 From an economic standpoint, it is necessary for me to engage in paid consulting work   51

FIGURE 34 My job is a source of considerable personal strain.   51

FIGURE 35 At this institution, how would you evaluate the technology for teaching?   52

FIGURE 36 At this institution, how would you evaluate the research equipment and instruments?   52

FIGURE 37 At this institution, how would you evaluate the computer facilities?   53

FIGURE 38 At this institution, how would you evaluate the library holdings?   53

FIGURE 39 This is an especially creative and productive time in my field.   54

FIGURE 40 To what extent are you satisfied with the courses you teach?   54

FIGURE 41 To what extent are you satisfied with the opportunity to pursue your own ideas?   55

FIGURE 42 To what extent are you satisfied with your relationships with colleagues?   55

FIGURE 43 Based on your experience at this institution, how would you assess the intellectual atmosphere?   56

FIGURE 44 This is a poor time for any young person to begin an academic career in my field.   56

FIGURE 45 If I had it to do over again, I would not become an academic.   57

FIGURE 46 How influential are you, personally, in helping to shape key academic policies at the institutional level?   57

FIGURE 47 Based on your experience at this institution, how would you assess relationships between faculty and administration?   58

FIGURE 48 I am kept informed about what is going on at this institution.   58

FIGURE 49 Communication between the faculty and the administration is poor.   59

FIGURE 50 The administration is often autocratic.   59

FIGURE 51 Lack of faculty involvement is a real problem.   60

FIGURE 52 Top-level administrators are providing competent leadership.   60

FIGURE 53 The administration supports academic freedom.   61

FIGURE 54   The government should have the responsibility to define the overall purposes and policies for higher education.   61

FIGURE 55   In this country, there is far too much governmental interference in important academic policies.   62

FIGURE 56   Is academic freedom strongly protected in this country?   62

FIGURE 57   I can focus my research on any topic of special interest to me.   63

FIGURE 58   At this institution, I am fully free to determine the content of the courses I teach.   63

FIGURE 59   In this country, there are no political or ideological restrictions on what a scholar may publish.   64

FIGURE 60   Respect for academics is declining.   64

FIGURE 61   Academics are among the most influential opinion leaders in my country.   65

FIGURE 62   Faculty in my discipline have a professional obligation to apply their knowledge to problems in society.   65

FIGURE 63   During the past three years at this institution, how frequently have foreign students been enrolled?   66

FIGURE 64   During the past three years at this institution, how frequently have your students studied abroad?   66

FIGURE 65   The curriculum at this institution should be more international in focus.   67

FIGURE 66   For how many months, during the past three years, have you travelled abroad to study or do research?   67

FIGURE 67   For how many months, during the past three years, have you served as a faculty member at an institution in another country?   68

FIGURE 68   In order to keep up with developments in my discipline, a scholar must read books and journals published abroad.   68

FIGURE 69   Connections with scholars in other countries are very important to my professional work.   69

FIGURE 70   A scholar's international connections are important in faculty evaluation at this institution.   69

LIST OF TABLES

TABLE 1   What is your gender?   73

TABLE 2   How old are you?   73

TABLE 3   At how many different institutions of higher education have you ever held a regular academic appointment?   74

TABLE 4   Is your current employment at this institution full time or part time?   74

TABLE 5   Do you currently hold other paid academic positions outside this institution?   75

TABLE 6   Do you currently hold other paid nonacademic positions outside this institution?   75

TABLE 7   Of your total earned income, what percentage comes from this institution?   76

TABLE 8   In your opinion, what percentage of the young people in your country are capable of completing secondary education?   76

TABLE 9   In your opinion, what percentage of students in your country who complete secondary education should be admitted to higher education?   77

TABLE 10   Access to higher education should be available to all who meet minimum entrance requirements.   77

TABLE 11   Admission standards should be lowered to permit disadvantaged students to enroll at this institution.   78

TABLE 12   The undergraduates you teach at this institution are adequately prepared in written and oral communication skills.   78

TABLE 13   The undergraduates you teach at this institution are adequately prepared in mathematics and quantitative reasoning skills.   79

TABLE 14   How would you rate the quality of the students currently enrolled in your department?   79

TABLE 15	Please indicate the degree to which your affiliation with your academic discipline is important to you.	80
TABLE 16	Please indicate the degree to which your affiliation with this institution is important to you.	80
TABLE 17	Regarding your own preferences, do your interests lie primarily in teaching or in research?	81
TABLE 18	The pressure to publish reduces the quality of teaching at this institution.	81
TABLE 19	Have you or your research group received any grants or special funding in the last three years?	82
TABLE 20	Please estimate the total amount of research funding you or your research group received in the last three years.	82
TABLE 21	Research funding in my field is easier to get now than it was five years ago.	83
TABLE 22	A strong record of successful research activity is important in faculty evaluation at this institution.	83
TABLE 23	In my department, it is difficult for a person to achieve tenure if he or she does not publish.	84
TABLE 24	I frequently feel under pressure to do more research than I actually would like to do.	84
TABLE 25	Which of these activities are appraised or evaluated regularly?	85
TABLE 26	Student opinions should be used in evaluating the teaching effectiveness of faculty.	85
TABLE 27	By whom is your teaching regularly evaluated?	86
TABLE 28	At this institution, we need better ways to evaluate teaching performance.	86
TABLE 29	At this institution, publications used for promotion decisions are just "counted," not qualitatively evaluated.	87
TABLE 30	How would you rate your own academic salary?	87
TABLE 31	From an economic standpoint, it is necessary for me to engage in paid consulting work.	88
TABLE 32	My job is a source of considerable personal strain.	88
TABLE 33	At this institution, how would you evaluate the technology for teaching?	89

TABLE 34	At this institution, how would you evaluate the research equipment and instruments? 89
TABLE 35	At this institution, how would you evaluate the computer facilities? 90
TABLE 36	At this institution, how would you evaluate the library holdings? 90
TABLE 37	This is an especially creative and productive time in my field. 91
TABLE 38	To what extent are you satisfied with the courses you teach? 91
TABLE 39	To what extent are you satisfied with the opportunity to pursue your own ideas? 92
TABLE 40	To what extent are you satisfied with your relationships with colleagues? 92
TABLE 41	Based on your experience at this institution, how would you assess the intellectual atmosphere? 93
TABLE 42	This is a poor time for any young person to begin an academic career in my field. 93
TABLE 43	If I had it to do over again, I would not become an academic. 94
TABLE 44	How influential are you, personally, in helping to shape key academic policies at the institutional level? 94
TABLE 45	Based on your experience at this institution, how would you assess relationships between faculty and administration? 95
TABLE 46	I am kept informed about what is going on at this institution. 95
TABLE 47	Communication between the faculty and the administration is poor. 96
TABLE 48	The administration is often autocratic. 96
TABLE 49	Lack of faculty involvement is a real problem. 97
TABLE 50	Top-level administrators are providing competent leadership. 97
TABLE 51	The administration supports academic freedom. 98
TABLE 52	The government should have the responsibility to define the overall purposes and policies for higher education. 98

TABLE 53	In this country there is far too much governmental interference in important academic policies. 99
TABLE 54	Is academic freedom strongly protected in this country? 99
TABLE 55	I can focus my research on any topic of special interest to me. 100
TABLE 56	At this institution, I am fully free to determine the content of the courses I teach. 100
TABLE 57	In this country, there are no political or ideological restrictions on what a scholar may publish. 101
TABLE 58	Respect for academics is declining. 101
TABLE 59	Academics are among the most influential opinion leaders in my country. 102
TABLE 60	Faculty in my discipline have a professional obligation to apply their knowledge to problems in society. 102
TABLE 61	During the past three years at this institution, how frequently have foreign students been enrolled? 103
TABLE 62	During the past three years at this institution, how frequently have your students studied abroad? 103
TABLE 63	The curriculum at this institution should be more international in focus. 104
TABLE 64	For how many months during the past three years have you travelled abroad to study or do research? 104
TABLE 65	For how many months during the past three years have you served as a faculty member at an institution in another country? 105
TABLE 66	In order to keep up with developments in my discipline, a scholar must read books and journals published abroad. 105
TABLE 67	Connections with scholars in other countries are very important to my professional work. 106
TABLE 68	A scholar's international connections are important in faculty evaluation at this institution. 106

ACKNOWLEDGMENTS

THIS REPORT IS THE RESULT of the first *international* survey conducted by The Carnegie Foundation. The project, unique for the Foundation in its scope, required the work and special dedication of many people.

First of all, I must thank Philip G. Altbach for advising the project. I am indebted to Phil for his wisdom and expertise in international higher education. Phil drew on his worldwide network of colleagues to help us assemble a remarkable team of scholars for the study. Phil's diplomacy and good judgment have helped immensely to keep this enormously complicated effort on track.

Mary Jean Whitelaw, technical director for the project, contributed integrally to the planning and design of the survey, and to the management, analysis, and interpretation of the data. Mary Jean's extensive experience in questionnaire design and survey methodology was invaluable in establishing the framework for this study, and in helping solve the many unique problems inevitable in a project of this scope. Her cooperative spirit and capacity to work calmly under pressure were essential to the project's success.

I owe a special debt to the members of our international research team. Without their commitment, cooperation, and contributions at every stage, this study would not have been possible. Their knowledge of higher education both at home and abroad is reflected in every facet of the work, from the survey instrument itself, to its administration in each country, to detailed summaries and critical analyses reporting the results.

This distinguished group of scholars included Barry Sheehan and Tony Welch, Australia; Simon Schwartzman and Elizabeth Balbachevsky, Brazil; Ernesto Schiefelbein, Chile; Anwar Mohamed El-Sharkawy and

Mohamed Mohieddin, Egypt; Ulrich Teichler and Jurgen Enders, Germany; Gerard Postiglione, Hong Kong; Michael Chen, Esther Gottlieb, and Ruth Yakir, Israel; Akira Arimoto, Japan; Sungho Lee, Korea; Manuel Gil Anton, Mexico; Frans van Vught and Peter Maassen, the Netherlands; Alexander Savelyev, Russia; Thorsten Nybom, Karsen Lundequist, and Hans Jalling, Sweden; Oliver Fulton, the United Kingdom; and Gene Haas, the United States.

Gene Haas played a dual role. Not only was he responsible for directing the survey in the United States, but he also designed the methodology and coordinated the administration of the survey in other countries with the international research directors. Gene's many contributions were informed by his long experience and a keen and creative sociological eye.

Other colleagues working within the Foundation also deserve special thanks. Mary Huber helped in the design and direction of the study from the beginning, and provided timely assistance in preparing the final report. Lois Harwood helped in designing the survey instrument, administering the study, and planning and coordinating the meetings of the international research team. She was instrumental in writing the intricate programs required to generate the tables and charts.

I am grateful to Craig Wacker, whose foreign language skills were a great asset in managing data as it came in, and who also helped with the computer programming and the production of tabular displays. Other colleagues lending assistance with the survey data were Dale Coye, Jacob Greenberg, Jan Hempel, Shannon Lucas, and Sarah White.

Lee Mitgang helped develop the framework on which this report is based, and his participation contributed greatly to the success of our second meeting of the research directors. Jeanine Natriello, with consummate grace and skill, organized and coordinated both of our international conferences, and Hinda Greenberg, director of the Foundation's Information Center, provided invaluable support and professional service throughout the project's life.

For work in the last stages of writing and editing this report, I thank Carolyn Lieberg. Jan Hempel edited the final manuscript, and oversaw its design and production.

Robert Hochstein's wise advice and counsel have been invaluable throughout. James Perkins participated in initial discussions and has continued to provide valuable comment and critique. Charles Glassick and Vito Perrone also made splendid contributions in the project's early days. Toward the end, we benefitted from Lionel Lewis's careful reading of the manuscript.

I am always indebted to the word processing skills of Dawn Ott and Laura Bell. Their speed and precision are outdone only by their ability to decipher illegible handwriting. Dawn also provided valuable assistance with the international conferences.

Without the generous financial assistance of the Andrew W. Mellon Foundation, The International Survey of the Academic Profession would not have been possible. In addition, partial funding for survey work was provided by agencies in several of the participating countries. I am indeed grateful for this support.

Finally, the success of this study has depended entirely on the good will of the thousands of professors worldwide who took the time to respond with care and consideration to our long and detailed questionnaire.

This has truly been an international team effort, and I am enormously grateful to all of these colleagues for their sacrificial and creative work.

ERNEST L. BOYER
President
The Carnegie Foundation
for the Advancement of Teaching

INTRODUCTION

The International Professoriate: An Overview

FOR SEVERAL DECADES, The Carnegie Foundation for the Advancement of Teaching has surveyed the American academic profession. The information we've gathered through the years has provided valuable insights into the attitudes and working conditions of the professoriate in the United States.

More efficient travel and communication, as well as a growing convergence of intellectual interests, have fostered in recent years a stronger, more professionally connected, international community of scholars. Those in the natural sciences, especially, have benefited from new collaborations. But increased intellectual exchange also has occurred among scholars in the social sciences and in the humanities, while those in the arts continue to communicate powerfully across borders. These connections have contributed richly to the work of the academy and have expanded the world's reservoir of knowledge.

Given this increased globalization of scholarly work, we concluded that the time had come to conduct the Foundation's first international study of the academic profession. Our goal was to learn more about the condition of the professoriate from a larger perspective and, in the process, define priorities that could strengthen the academy worldwide.

After consulting with colleagues both here and overseas, we developed a research procedure and gathered information about the academic profession in many countries.[1] The result is, we believe, the most compre-

---

[1] The countries included in this report are Australia, Brazil, Chile, Germany, Hong Kong, Israel, Japan, Korea, Mexico, the Netherlands, Russia, Sweden, the United Kingdom, and the United States.

hensive view of the professoriate available today. With the information we've gathered, it is possible to understand more fully both similarities and differences among academics around the world.

There are, we found, variations on such important matters as student access, teaching and research, and support for academic freedom. On the other hand, there are striking similarities among faculty regarding the need for better methods of evaluating teaching, a commitment to service to help solve societal problems, as well as concern over the governance of higher education.

We have organized our findings around seven major themes that could provide an agenda for policy consideration. They are: the profile of the professoriate; access to higher education; professional activities; working conditions of faculty; governing the academy; higher education and society; and the international dimensions of academic life. Before discussing each of these in more detail, we present here in brief some of the highlights of our study.

First, we found, not surprisingly, that the majority of faculty worldwide are male and middle-aged. And while most professors hold full-time appointments, in a few countries we found a sizable minority in part-time positions.

Regarding student access, most faculty believe that higher education should be available to everyone who meets the minimum qualifications, but they do not think admission standards should be lowered to admit disadvantaged students. We found widespread agreement among faculty that students currently enrolled are ill prepared in language and math skills.

When we asked about the historic missions of teaching, research, and service, we found differences from one country to another. The majority of professors in several countries say they prefer teaching, while the majority in other countries prefer research. We also discovered that in almost all countries a strong record of successful research is important for faculty advancement, even though a surprising percentage of the faculty say that, at their institution, research publications are "just counted," not qualitatively evaluated.

A number of the survey questions asked about faculty working conditions. We found notable differences among the countries, including, for example, the economic need for faculty to do outside consulting work. On the other hand, we also found points of agreement. Faculty in many countries are concerned about their salary, and a surprisingly large number say that their jobs are a source of considerable personal strain. Faculty in many nations also feel that institutional resources are inadequate.

On the positive side, professors reported a high sense of satisfaction with their intellectual lives, with the courses they teach, and with their relationships with colleagues. Many academics around the world also believe this is a good time to become a scholar. And the great majority say they would become an academic if they had it to do over again.

Our survey also examined the control of higher education. In some nations, colleges and universities are government-controlled, while in others there is a strong tradition of institutional independence. These contrasting traditions are reflected in faculty responses to questions about government's role in defining the overall purposes of higher education and the degree to which government involvement has become excessive.

Regarding campus governance, we found that in most countries relatively few faculty believe top administrators are providing competent leadership. Many report that communication between faculty and administration is poor, and faculty worldwide feel that they are less influential in their institutions.

No issue is of greater concern to the world of scholarship than academic freedom, and we found that, in most countries, faculty have confidence that, nationally, this freedom is protected. However, in only a few countries do a majority of professors feel that academic freedom is supported by campus administrators, and in some countries, including the United States, a significant minority feel political or ideological constraints on what a scholar may publish.

A growing concern in many countries is how higher learning relates to the larger society. Around the world, there is pressure for academics to contribute more tangibly to economic development and social well-being, and when we asked professors whether faculty in their discipline do, in fact, have a professional obligation to apply their knowledge to problems in society, the response was emphatically affirmative. At the same time, however, we discovered that service activities are not regularly evaluated in most countries.

Finally, we studied the degree to which an international community of scholarship is, in fact, emerging. Professors overwhelmingly maintain that connections with scholars in other countries are very important to their professional work. We found as well a strong commitment to exchange activities—students and faculty studying abroad, and an awareness of the importance of scholarly materials published elsewhere. All of this suggests that within the academy national boundaries are becoming blurred.

These then are among the highlights of our study. The following chapters explore in more detail the seven themes covered by the report and offer suggestions for a future international policy agenda for higher education.

CHAPTER I

Profile of the Professoriate

OUR INQUIRY FOCUSED FIRST on a profile of the professoriate. In all countries most academics are men. However, regional variations in this pattern are striking. The highest proportion of male faculty—around 90 percent—is found in Japan and Korea, while in Australia and the American countries of the United States, Chile, Mexico, and Brazil, it is 60 to 70 percent. The proportion in European countries, Hong Kong, and Israel falls in between.

In the United States, progress has been made through the years toward greater gender equity. In 1969, the percentage of women holding academic positions was 19 percent.[1] Today, according to our survey, it is 30 percent. Still, the academic profession worldwide remains disproportionately male, reflecting the relatively recent admission of women into the faculty in many countries and the continuing barriers they face in negotiating academic careers.

The professoriate is a middle aged profession. In most countries, the average age is between forty and fifty years. Here again the pattern varies, with Mexico having the youngest faculty (averaging under forty years) and Israel, Japan, and Russia, the oldest (over fifty).

The mobility of faculty is of special interest. Most professors have taught at only one or two institutions. However, over one-fourth of the faculty in Hong Kong, Australia, Brazil, Israel, and the United States have worked at three or more institutions during the course of their careers. Mobility was lowest in Korea and Russia.

In all countries, a majority of faculty are employed full time at their

---

[1] Survey of Faculty and Student Opinion, 1969, by the Carnegie Commission on Higher Education and the American Council on Education.

college or university, but in Brazil, Mexico, and Chile, significant numbers are employed part time. Over one-quarter of respondents in the Latin American countries and in Israel and Japan hold additional academic positions. Also in Latin America, over one-third of professors hold outside nonacademic jobs. In fact, in Brazil, Mexico, and Chile, faculty earn an average of over 20 percent of their total income from extra academic and nonacademic work.

The demographic profile of today's professoriate raises questions about the future of the profession. What, for instance, can be done to increase the opportunities for academic employment for women worldwide? With a faculty that is aging but still far from retirement, what opportunities are available for younger scholars?

Research directors in many countries reported that the number of part-timers seems to be growing, and a recent report from the American Association of University Professors[2] concludes that part-time faculty hold 38 percent of faculty appointments in the United States. The implications of these developments are surely of great consequence to the academy in all countries. Will the academic profession follow a Latin American model, where significant proportions of faculty hold part-time positions? Will increasing numbers of scholars feel pressured to augment their salaries from other academic and nonacademic work? Responses to these questions in the days ahead will have a profound impact on the international community of scholars.

---

[2] American Association of University Professors, "The Status of Non-Tenure-Track Faculty," Academe, July–August 1993, pp. 39–46.

CHAPTER II

Students: Access and Excellence

WE CONSIDERED NEXT the essential issue of student access. Following World War II, enrollment policies shifted in most countries—earliest and most dramatically in the United States, which moved almost overnight from "elite" to "mass" higher education. Today, more than 60 percent of high school graduates go on to higher education, and the number is climbing.[1] And it's widely accepted in the United States that to succeed economically and socially, young people need a college education.

Outside the United States, even the most elite higher education systems have in recent years expanded access. Yet little effort has been made to determine faculty attitudes about this fundamental shift in policy that affects so profoundly the climate of the campus and the work of the professoriate. We decided, therefore, to ask faculty how they feel about access. How many students who complete secondary education should be admitted to higher education? Should admission requirements be modified to achieve greater equity, and how do professors feel about students already enrolled? Are today's students academically well prepared?

Overall, faculty in most countries believe that a majority of their young people can complete secondary education. Of those students who do complete it, faculty opinion is that perhaps one-half should be admitted to higher education. There are, however, notable differences from one nation to another. In Russia, for example, faculty think that

---

[1] In 1991, 62.4 percent of high school graduates enrolled in college. National Center for Education Statistics, U.S. Department of Education, Office of Educational Research and Improvement, *Digest of Education Statistics*, 1992, p. 183.

only about 30 percent of secondary school graduates should go on to higher learning, while German faculty say 73 percent should continue their studies. It is important to note, however, that German professors also feel that less than 40 percent of the young people in their country are capable of completing *secondary* education.

Perhaps one of the most significant policy issues to be confronted is higher education's commitment to diversity. In all countries except the Netherlands, over 50 percent of faculty agree that higher education should be available to all who meet minimum entrance requirements. However, except in Australia, we did not find strong support for the idea of lowering admission standards to serve disadvantaged students.

Overall, professors are understandably reluctant to lower admission standards, especially in light of their current dissatisfaction with student preparation. Less than one-third of the faculty in most countries say their students are adequately prepared in writing and communication skills. Indeed in five of these countries, including the United States, it is 20 percent or less. Also, in most nations, only a small proportion of professors report that students are adequately prepared in mathematics, with professors in the United States being the least satisfied, and professors in Hong Kong the most.

A somewhat brighter picture emerged when we asked faculty about the quality of students currently enrolled in their departments. Even here, however, fewer than half the professors in many of the countries rated their students "good" or "excellent."

We did note, with interest, that over 60 percent of faculty in the United States rated students in their department "good" or "excellent." How can this be explained, especially given the low opinion faculty in this country have about the pre-college preparation of undergraduates? One possibility is that faculty judge their "majors"—advanced students enrolled in their departments—more favorably than they do other students. There is, in short, a selectivity involved, and students, having moved into a field of special interest, may be more motivated and successful.

Looking ahead, it seems safe to predict that access to college will increase in response to the continuing revolution of rising expectations.

Students and their parents in all countries will, we believe, continue to view college as the ladder to success, and higher education will feel pressure to expand. But will public policy and funding support such growth? Given increasing access, how can collaboration be strengthened between higher learning and the schools? And how does a more egalitarian policy in enrollment relate to a more elitist view of the professoriate that does not adequately reward teaching or counseling? Finally, what are the implications for the curriculum as student populations become more diverse?

These issues should be thoughtfully considered by the academy as higher learning seeks to extend its commitment to sustain excellence while affirming social equity. Where, in fact, should the balance be struck?

CHAPTER III

Professional Activity: Teaching, Research, and Service

WE FOCUSED WITH SPECIAL INTENSITY on the nature of academic work. In many countries there has been growing concern in recent years about how professors spend their time, a debate that has involved discussions about "productivity" and most especially about the relationships among teaching, research, and professional service.

At the heart of the matter is the commitment faculty feel toward their discipline, on the one hand, and toward their institution on the other. We discovered that, in every country, a larger majority of faculty say their academic discipline is "very important" to them. Only in three nations—all in Latin America—do a significant number say their *institution* is "very important" to them, while in the other countries, more indicate that the institution is only "fairly important." Overall, it seems quite clear that the orientation of the academy is more cosmopolitan than local: *professional* loyalty is stronger than *campus* loyalty.

When we asked faculty to indicate whether they prefer teaching or research, national differences appeared. Commitment to teaching predominates in five of the fourteen countries, with Russia leading at 68 percent, followed closely by the four American countries, all over 60 percent. In the nine other countries, faculty interest leans to research, with the Netherlands leading at 76 percent.

Still, the majority of faculty in all countries, except Hong Kong, do not agree that the pressure to publish reduces the quality of teaching. A conflict is felt, however, by a significant minority in Australia, Germany, the United States, the Netherlands, Israel, the United Kingdom, and Chile.

Faculty *do* have other concerns about research. For one thing, funding is not always available. Over half the respondents in most countries did receive some funding for their research, but the support level was modest. Further, faculty feel that money for research is more difficult to obtain now than it was five years ago. This perception is most acute in Russia, the United Kingdom, the United States, and Germany.

A solid proportion of professors in all countries except Russia and Korea report that a strong research record is important in faculty evaluation. Indeed, in six countries, a majority say it is difficult to achieve tenure without publication. And a strong minority in several countries feel pressure to do more research than they would like to do.

How to evaluate academic work is of high interest internationally. At least two-thirds of the professors in all nations, except Germany and Japan, note that teaching is evaluated regularly. In most countries, research activities are somewhat less regularly appraised. Service, however, is seldom evaluated, except in the United States.

A large majority of professors in most countries agree that student opinions should be used in the evaluation of teaching effectiveness. And in fact, more than 90 percent of the faculty in Sweden and the United States report that students do regularly evaluate their teaching. Only in Japan and Korea do less than half of faculty report that students regularly evaluate teaching.

Still, we found widespread dissatisfaction with faculty evaluation. Replies from all countries overwhelmingly indicate that better ways are needed to evaluate teaching performance. Many academics have doubts about research evaluation, too. In ten of twelve countries, for example, more than 40 percent of the faculty agree that publications used for promotion decisions at their institutions are just "counted," not qualitatively evaluated. Sweden and Israel were strong exceptions.

It's clear that educators in all countries must think carefully about the missions of the academy, broadening the definition of scholarship, affirming diversity in higher education, and celebrating a mosaic of faculty talent. In the process, performance standards must be broadened. And we believe that teaching must, once again, be recognized as an essential function of the professoriate and be well rewarded.

CHAPTER IV

Working Conditions: Satisfactions and Frustrations

THE WORKING CONDITIONS of faculty, inevitably, influence both productivity and morale, and we were interested in exploring sources of satisfaction and frustration. We found that most faculty feel they are not well paid. Indeed, in only two places—Hong Kong and the Netherlands—do more than half the faculty rate their own salary as "good" or "excellent." In the United States, 46 percent rate their salaries this favorably. In six countries, only 15 percent or less of the faculty report such satisfaction.

In some nations, faculty have turned to paid consulting to supplement their salaries. This is especially true in Russia, where more than 80 percent agree that outside work is essential. But over half the faculty in Korea and in the Latin American countries also report that supplementary work is necessary. Looking down the road, one wonders if this trend will continue.

The professoriate is in many respects a privileged career group. Still, much of the faculty feel under pressure. In nearly half the responding countries, 40 percent or more say their job is a source of considerable personal strain. Japanese, Russian, and Korean faculty report the most pressure. In the United States one-third feel considerable pressure from their work. But in Israel less than 20 percent say their job is a source of strain.

Faculty also are rather dissatisfied with the resources available for teaching and research at their institutions. Replies did, however, vary remarkably among countries. Asked to rate such facilities as instructional technology, research equipment, computer facilities, and library holdings, five countries came out consistently at the top: Hong Kong, the Netherlands, the United States, Sweden, and Germany. If these countries form the "haves," professors in Russia, Japan, and Korea are the "have nots," except in reported library holdings. Overall, faculty tend to rate computer facilities and library resources more favorably than technology for teaching and research.

Frustrations notwithstanding, professors around the world report intellectual satisfaction in their work. In all but three countries, 60 percent or more of the faculty agree that this is an especially creative and productive time in their field. Further, they are generally satisfied with the courses they teach and, with a few notable exceptions, are pleased with the opportunities they have to pursue their own ideas.

In general, professors are also satisfied with their relationships with colleagues, and in most countries the majority find the intellectual atmosphere at their institution good. Only a third of the faculty feel this is a poor time for a young person to begin a career in their field. And overwhelmingly, professors say they would become an academic if they had it to do over. It would be especially interesting, we believe, to explore why faculty around the world define this as an intellectually creative time. What are the reasons for this assessment, and how can this quality be extended and enhanced?

We note with satisfaction that most faculty are encouraged by prospects in their field and pleased about their own career choice. And the fact that faculty are generally satisfied with their courses and with their opportunities to explore intellectually interesting issues is, we believe, strong ground upon which to build communities of scholarship, both on campus and beyond.

At the same time, one wonders about the personal strain among professors. How much does it reflect financial worries? How much does it involve frustration over inadequate facilities and technical support? How much does it reflect the contradictory signals faculty are often given about the value of their work? If colleges and universities are to meet the expectations societies hold for the academy, signals sent to faculty about priorities must be clear.

CHAPTER V

Governing the Academy

How universities govern themselves remains one of the most confusing, most tension-ridden issues in higher education, and the type of governance differs dramatically from one country to another.

Throughout the world, faculty dissatisfaction with current arrangements is high. The majority of faculty in all nations except Japan and Brazil say they are "not at all influential" in helping to shape key academic policies at the institutional level.

In addition, faculty in most countries feel alienated from top administrators at their institutions. Half or more say that relationships between faculty and administration are only "fair" or "poor"—with Korea and Japan the least content. In general, fewer than half the faculty feel they are kept informed about what is going on, and about half say communication between faculty and administration is "poor."

In eight countries, most faculty believe that the administration at their institution is "autocratic." In six countries, a majority agree that "lack of faculty involvement" is a problem.

Overall, faculty believe administrators are not doing a very good job. In most countries, fewer than one-third are satisfied with the leadership of top level administrators at their universities. Japan is the only country in which a majority of scholars agree that top administrators are providing competent leadership. What's most disturbing, perhaps, is that only in Israel, Japan, the United States, and Brazil do more than half the faculty feel that administrators support academic freedom.

What might be the reasons for this widespread dissatisfaction? One possibility is that as higher education dramatically expanded to accommodate increasing numbers of students, colleges and universities developed a hierarchical "industrial model" of governance. Layers of administrators were created to handle everything from personnel policies to facilities to financial aid. Faculty, organized administratively into academic divisions and departments, became more and more removed from issues affecting the institution as a whole. Decisions emanating from afar often seemed at odds with daily realities, creating within the institution a climate of confusion and sometimes distrust.

Worldwide, governance arrangements in universities and colleges which increased "efficiency" also reduced communication and collegiality, becoming a clear source of faculty frustration. How can the governance of higher education be improved and collegiality strengthened? Is it possible to increase the quality of discourse by bringing together professors and administrators to solve pressing issues while fostering mutual trust and respect? What can faculty from various countries learn from one another regarding governance?

CHAPTER VI

Higher Education and Society

COLLEGES AND UNIVERSITIES are deeply embedded in the societies they serve. An issue of special focus in this study was the health of that relationship. Do scholars have academic freedom? What respect is assigned to professors, and how do academics, in turn, extend their work into society at large? Finally, is the integrity of higher learning being sustained?

Since some universities are publicly controlled while others are independent, it is hardly surprising that differences exist among countries in the relationship between government and higher education. When we asked faculty whether government should define the overall policies for higher education, affirmative replies ranged from a high of 90 percent in Russia to a low of 10 percent in the United States, with other countries clustering at the 40 percent level. When asked if government interferes too much in important academic policies, about 90 percent of the faculty in Korea agree. In Chile only 17 percent agree. In the United States one-third agree.

In reviewing these data we are left with key questions: In balancing national and international goals, what should be government's role in shaping the overall policy for higher education? What issues are of legitimate *public* concern? And how can an appropriate balance be struck between shaping national policy and maintaining the independence of the academy?

No issue is more crucial to the professoriate than academic freedom. And with the exception of Russia and Brazil, most faculty feel such freedom is strongly protected in their country. Also large majorities in every country say they are free to do research on any topic of special interest, and—with the exception of Russia—to determine the content of the courses they teach. In Korea and the United States, however, more than one-third feel there are political or ideological restrictions on what a scholar can publish. This is a disturbing trend, perhaps reflecting governmental oversight in Korea and "political correctness" pressure in the United States. Will such pressures become a dominant force elsewhere?

Another matter of concern is the respect academics feel they receive in their own nation. The overall pattern of responses is not encouraging. About 60 percent of faculty overall feel respect for academics is declining in their country—ranging from nearly 80 percent in Brazil to around 40 percent in the Netherlands and Sweden. We also asked, "Are academics among the most influential opinion leaders in your country?" Professors in Korea perceive a higher level of influence. Those in the United Kingdom perceive the least.

We are encouraged, however, by the attitude of faculty toward professional service. Specifically, we asked faculty to agree or disagree with this statement: "Faculty in my discipline have a professional obligation to apply their knowledge to problems in society." The response was overwhelmingly affirmative—ranging from over 90 percent in Germany to 61 percent in Russia. In the United States it is more than 80 percent. These figures reflect, we believe, the faculty's confidence in the practical value of their knowledge and their concern about larger social issues.

CHAPTER VII

The International Dimension

THERE IS A LOT OF TALK THESE DAYS about "internationalizing" higher education, but to what extent is this actually occurring? How important are international connections to faculty? How do they feel about such collaboration? And to what degree are faculty and students already communicating across national lines?

We found that in all countries except Korea, close to 50 percent or more of faculty, at least occasionally, report that foreign students have been enrolled at their institutions. The United States is the highest. In this country, virtually all faculty members report that their institutions recently have been host to foreign students. The proportion of faculty saying that their students study in other countries also is impressive, ranging from a high of 81 percent in Japan to a low of 12 percent in Korea.

Overall, professors believe the curriculum should be more international in focus. The exception is Israel, where only 29 percent support this idea. Next lowest are the United States and Australia, where faculty support for a more international curriculum is around 45 percent. Are curricula in these countries already international in focus? Or do these faculty believe their students get sufficient exposure to international issues in other ways?

In the past three years, over half the professors in ten countries made trips abroad to study or do research. The range was quite wide. Israel led the way, with over 90 percent of respondents studying abroad. Brazil, Russia, and the United States trail behind, with only about one-third. Fewer faculty spend time teaching in other nations, but 65 percent of Israeli professors say they have taught abroad in the past three years, followed by those from the Netherlands and Hong Kong. Fewer than 10 percent of faculty from the United States, Russia, Korea, Japan, and Brazil have recently taught overseas.

Faculty in all countries almost unanimously agree that they must read books or journal articles published abroad to keep up with developments in their discipline. Here again, the response was lowest in the United States. How is this to be interpreted? Is this because American professors are more parochial than those elsewhere? Or is it because this country is a worldwide center for academic publication?

Lastly, faculty also agree that connections with scholars in other countries are important for their professional work. And when asked whether an international connection is important in faculty evaluation, over 60 percent of the faculty in four countries—Israel, Japan, Sweden, and Chile—say yes. In Russia only about 20 percent agree.

It is especially encouraging to find a deep conviction among faculty that higher education is, in fact, an international enterprise and that the academic profession is becoming a global community. We are left with a series of vital questions: What will be the consequences of the new, electronic, international age, and how will the professoriate adapt? How will a newly connected "network of scholars" affect campus policy making? Will we, for example, see common procedures in the evaluation of scholarship? Will procedures regarding credits and courses and student evaluation begin to converge? In the days ahead, we anticipate that in all of these matters national boundaries will become less consequential to intellectual work.

CHAPTER VIII

Reflections: Prospects for the Future

THE GEOGRAPHIC LINES dividing the world of scholarship are becoming blurred. A global community of academic interests is emerging. Scholars everywhere, while maintaining national distinctions, acknowledge common concerns—not just intellectually but professionally as well. And in the century ahead, three critical issues will influence profoundly the shape and vitality of higher learning all around the world.

First, *student access*. Faculty members in most countries express a strong commitment to expanding opportunity. While cautiously concluding that not all young people in their countries are capable of completing secondary education, faculty strongly agree that access to higher education should be available to all who meet minimum entrance requirements. These expectations, which fall short of full access, still go far beyond current practice in most countries and reflect, we believe, a truly remarkable success story for the continued democratization of education.

At the same time, most faculty reject the idea of lowering academic standards to admit disadvantaged students. They also express frustration that college students are often inadequately prepared in the basic skills, indicating a continuing tension both here and abroad between access and excellence. Still, it's truly impressive that academics support the expansion of educational opportunities, which signals a continuing international movement from "elite" to "mass" higher education.

The second key issue is *governance*. In the years following World War II, a more complex, more bureaucratic administrative structure was established on campuses in many countries, most especially in the United States. It is argued that this "industrial model" of governance led to more efficiency and greater accountability in higher education. But the cost of these gains has been a breakdown in collegiality. Large numbers of faculty in many countries feel they are not influential in shaping academic policies at their institutions, are dissatisfied with the relationship between faculty and administration, and seem to distrust campus leadership.

In the 1960s, higher education faced a worldwide crisis of student alienation. Today, the crisis centers on ineffective governance arrangements. Frankly, it's difficult to imagine how universities can adjust creatively to changing times if academics and administrators do not communicate authentically with each other, not just about procedural matters, but about the larger purposes of the institution.

The third issue relates to *teaching, research, and service*. The continuing tension between classroom instruction and research persists, not only in the United States, but elsewhere, too. Clearly, the challenge is to move beyond the teaching *versus* research debate and give to scholarship a broader, more efficacious meaning, one that not only promotes the scholarship of *discovering* knowledge, but also the scholarship of *transmitting* knowledge in the classroom.

Finally, there is service. Today, professors all around the world support the idea of wider engagement. Overwhelmingly, they feel a professional obligation to apply their knowledge to the problems of society, building a bridge between theory and practice. Yet, ironically, in many countries professional service is not regularly evaluated, which may mean that professors who spend too much time applying their knowledge to real life issues could compromise their careers.

The United States is, occasionally, cited as an exception. Faculty on many campuses often engage in administrative and committee work, which is considered a form of "service." While such activity is of merit, it does not fulfill the larger vision of the scholarship of applying knowledge, which even in the United States usually goes unrewarded. And as a consequence of such detachment, the influence of the professoriate seems to be declining at the very time the need for academic engagement is most urgent.

These issues taken together—*student access, campus governance,* and *teaching, research, and service*—are of great consequence to higher education. The academy must consider these questions:

- How will institutions of higher learning achieve both access *and* excellence?
- How can the university reorganize itself to achieve both efficiency *and* collegiality?
- How can both teaching and research be appropriately recognized and rewarded?
- And how can scholars also harness their collective talents for the public good?

Fortunately, an international community of scholarship is, in fact, evolving. Faculty everywhere are traveling abroad, studying the scholarship from other countries, and consulting with colleagues through electronic highways that circle the globe. This international network of knowledge and exchange is increasing connections within and across disciplines and creating new forums that will improve higher education worldwide, strengthening the quality of society itself. Clearly, the intellectual resources of higher learning were never greater and never more needed than they are today.

TECHNICAL NOTES

WE DECIDED, EARLY ON, to include in our study countries that had rather well developed and well supported higher education systems. Faculty from all continents were included, and the only geographical region entirely absent is sub Saharan Africa. In the end, the following were selected: the United States; Germany[1], the Netherlands, Russia, Sweden, and the United Kingdom in Europe; Hong Kong, Japan, and Korea[2] in Asia; Brazil, Chile, and Mexico in Latin American; Egypt[3] and Israel in the Middle East; and Australia.

This study is unique not only because of its international perspective, but also because of the way it was conducted. Research directors from each participating country came together both to plan and to implement the project. While the questionnaire we used is based on The Carnegie Foundation's original format for surveys of college and university faculty in the United States, it was significantly modified to reflect the international context of the new study and to focus on new topics identified by the international research group. The very process of designing the questionnaire was itself a revealing exercise, as differences in priorities of the professoriate, and even the meanings of basic concepts, were discovered, debated, and resolved.

The twelve page questionnaire included over two hundred questions covering a wide variety of topics. A core of questions was used in every country. However, research directors could omit questions from their

---

[1] Only the former West Germany was included.
[2] Republic of Korea (South Korea).
[3] Due to technical problems, data from Egypt are not included in this report.

own country's survey instrument if the topic was not applicable or not relevant in their country. In some instances, countries added questions to reflect specific national circumstances.

The final questionnaire was translated into the languages of each country (Arabic, Dutch, German, Hebrew, Japanese, Korean, Portuguese, Russian, and Spanish; an English version was used in Australia, Hong Kong, Sweden, the United Kingdom, and the United States). Translated versions of the questionnaire were checked for accuracy and comparability in meaning using a process of back-translation.

A common method was used to select institutions and faculty respondents and to ensure a reliable random sample. The sampling methodology included a two-stage (in some cases, stratified) random sample. In the first stage, institutions were selected, and in the second stage, faculty names from these institutions were chosen.

Institutions awarding the baccalaureate degree or a higher degree were included in the universe from which institutions were selected. Two-year, technical, community, and junior colleges and their equivalent institutions around the world were not included in this study. Faculty were included in the universe if they had some teaching or research responsibilities at the selected institutions.

The questionnaires were distributed by mail in most countries, although in some countries questionnaires were distributed through the campus mail. In all countries the questionnaires were self administered. Each research director was asked to plan the sampling so that there would be at least one thousand usable responses. While the actual number of responses varied, they all fell within a range considered appropriate for survey studies of this kind.

Many of the figures included in this report reflect results to questions which include "agree," "neutral," and "disagree" response categories. The figures in this report show the proportion of respondents who reported "agree" or "disagree." It is important to remember that, in some cases, there may be a significant number of respondents who reported "neutral." If a respondent skipped a question, the answer was considered "missing" and any calculation of statistics relating to the question excludes the respondent entirely. Some tables and figures do not include the results from all the countries that asked a particular question. A review of the questions indicated that the phrasing or meaning of the questions was not identical and, therefore, comparing the results might be misleading.

A complete technical report describing the general design of the project as well as the specific details of the administration of the study in each country will be made available.

APPENDIX

MEMBERS OF THE RESEARCH TEAM for The Carnegie Foundation for the Advancement of Teaching's "International Survey of the Academic Profession, 1991–1993"

AUSTRALIA
Prof. Barry Sheehan, University of Melbourne
Dr. Anthony R. Welch, Faculty of Education, University of Sydney

BRAZIL
Prof. Simon Schwartzman, Research Center on Higher Education, University of Sao Paulo
Dr. Elizabeth Balbachevsky, Research Center on Higher Education, University of Sao Paulo

CHILE
Dr. Ernesto Schiefelbein, Minister of Education, Republic of Chile, Santiago, and UNESCO–OREALC, Santiago

EGYPT
Dr. Anwar Mohamed El-Sharkawy, Director, National Center for Educational Research and Development, Cairo (1991)
Dr. Mohamed M. Mohieddin, Social Research Center, American University in Cairo

GERMANY
Prof. Dr. Ulrich Teichler, Center for Higher Education and Work, Comprehensive University of Kassel

Dr. Jurgen Enders, Center for Higher Education and Work, Comprehensive University of Kassel

HONG KONG

Dr. Gerard Postiglione, Faculty of Education, University of Hong Kong

ISRAEL

Prof. Michael Chen, School of Education, University of Tel Aviv

Dr. Esther Gottlieb, State Teachers College–Seminar Hakibbutzim, Tel Aviv

Dr. Ruth Yakir, State Teachers College–Seminar Hakibbutzim, Tel Aviv

JAPAN

Prof. Akira Arimoto, Research Institute for Higher Education, Hiroshima National University

KOREA

Prof. Sungho Lee, School of Education, Yonsei University, Seoul, and former deputy Minister of Higher Education, Government of the Republic of Korea

MEXICO

Prof. Manuel Gil Anton, Universidad Antonoma Metropolitana, Unidad Azcapotzalco, Mexico City

NETHERLANDS

Prof. Frans van Vught, Center for Higher Education Policy Studies, University of Twente, Enschede

Prof. Peter Maassen, Center for Higher Education Policy Studies, University of Twente, Enschede

RUSSIA

Prof. Alexander Savelyev, Director, Russian Research Institute on Higher Education, Moscow

SWEDEN

Dr. Hans Jalling, Council for the Renewal of Undergraduate Education, Stockholm

Prof. Thorsten Nybom, Council for Studies on Higher Education, Stockholm

Dr. Karsen Lundequist, Council for Studies on Higher Education, Stockholm

UNITED KINGDOM

Prof. Oliver Fulton, Department of Educational Research, University of Lancaster

UNITED STATES

Dr. J. Eugene Haas, The Carnegie Foundation for the Advancement of Teaching, Princeton, New Jersey

CONSULTANT

Prof. Philip G. Altbach, School of Education, Boston College, Chestnut Hill, Massachusetts, and Senior Associate, The Carnegie Foundation for the Advancement of Teaching, Princeton, New Jersey

FIGURES

Figure 1

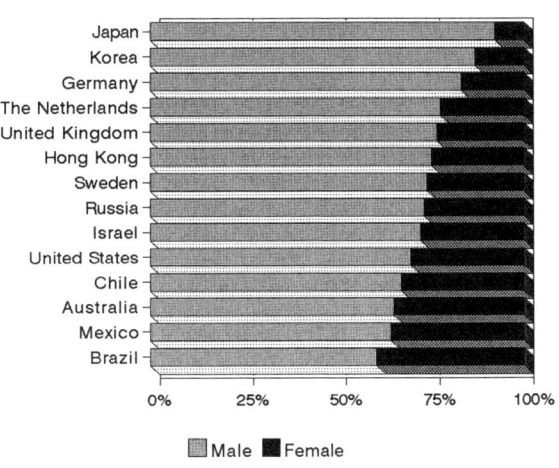

Figure 2

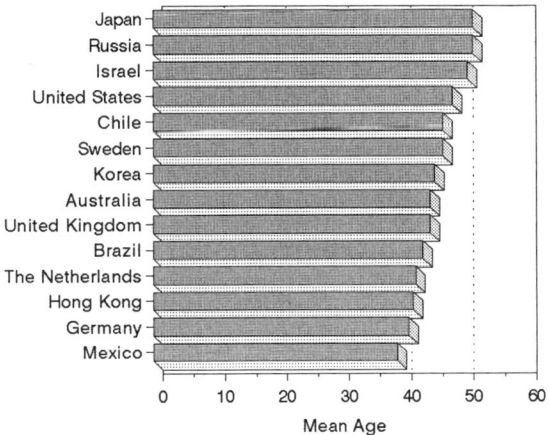

Figure 3

AT HOW MANY DIFFERENT INSTITUTIONS OF HIGHER EDUCATION HAVE YOU EVER HELD A REGULAR ACADEMIC APPOINTMENT?

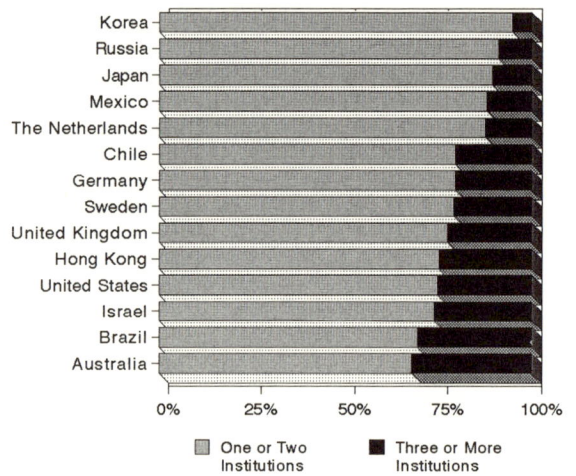

Figure 4

IS YOUR CURRENT EMPLOYMENT AT THIS INSTITUTION FULL TIME OR PART TIME?

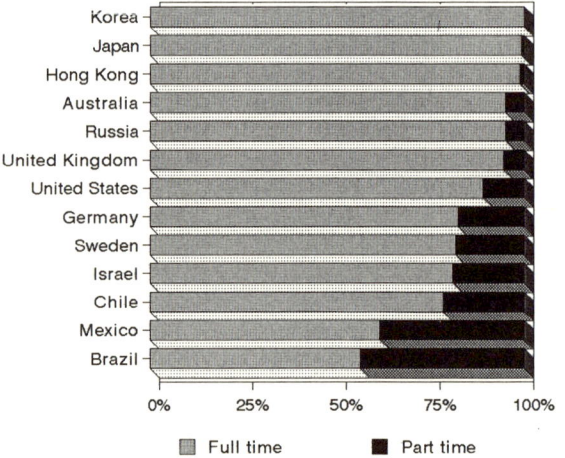

Figure 5

DO YOU CURRENTLY HOLD OTHER PAID ACADEMIC
POSITIONS OUTSIDE THIS INSTITUTION?
(Percentage Responding "Yes")

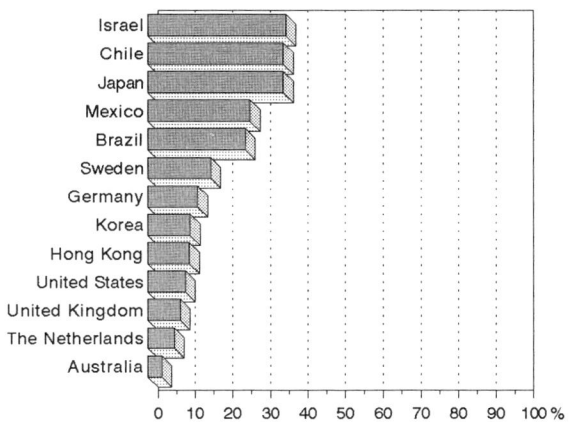

Figure 6

DO YOU CURRENTLY HOLD OTHER PAID NONACADEMIC
POSITIONS OUTSIDE THIS INSTITUTION?
(Percentage Responding "Yes")

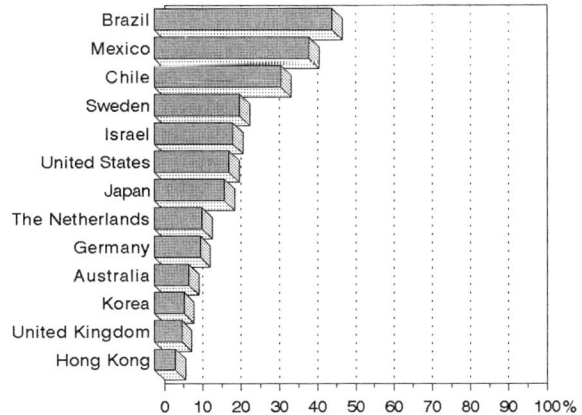

Figure 7
OF YOUR TOTAL EARNED INCOME, WHAT PERCENTAGE COMES FROM THIS INSTITUTION?

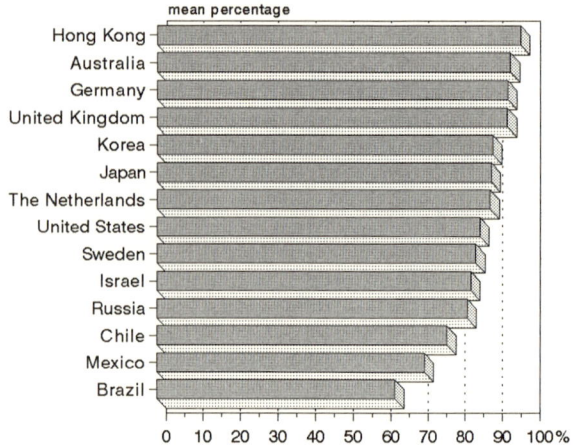

Figure 8
IN YOUR OPINION, WHAT PERCENTAGE OF THE YOUNG PEOPLE IN YOUR COUNTRY ARE CAPABLE OF COMPLETING SECONDARY EDUCATION?

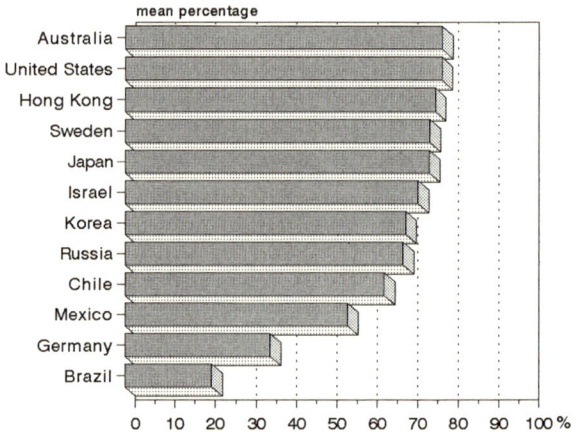

Figure 9
IN YOUR OPINION, WHAT PERCENTAGE OF STUDENTS IN YOUR COUNTRY WHO COMPLETE SECONDARY EDUCATION SHOULD BE ADMITTED TO HIGHER EDUCATION?

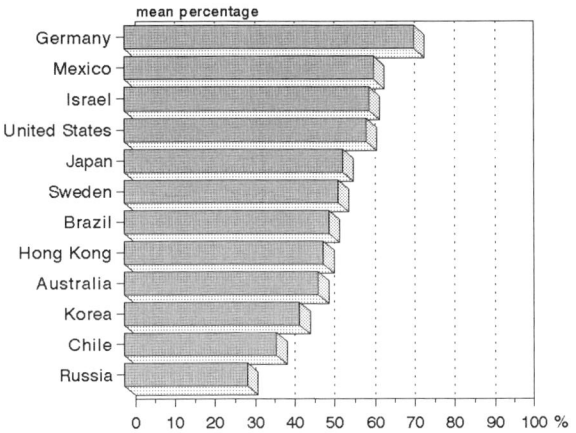

Figure 10
ACCESS TO HIGHER EDUCATION SHOULD BE AVAILABLE TO ALL WHO MEET MINIMUM ENTRANCE REQUIREMENTS.
(Percentage Agreeing)

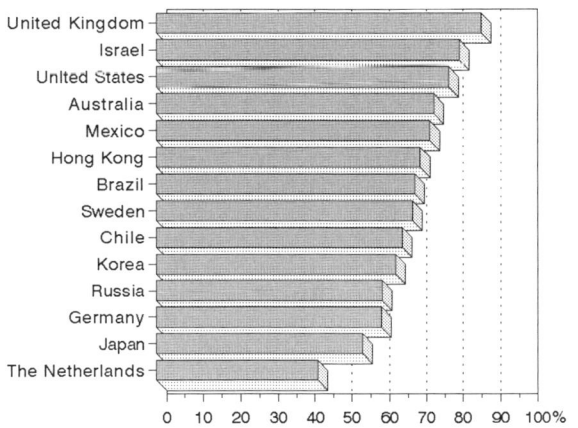

Figure 11

ADMISSION STANDARDS SHOULD BE LOWERED TO PERMIT DISADVANTAGED STUDENTS TO ENROLL AT THIS INSTITUTION.
(Percentage Agreeing)

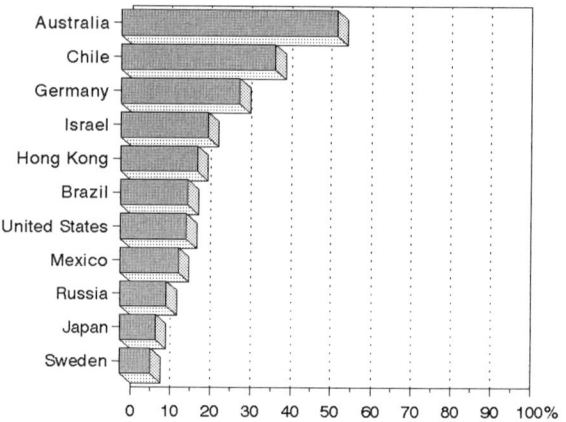

Figure 12

THE UNDERGRADUATES YOU TEACH AT THIS INSTITUTION ARE ADEQUATELY PREPARED IN WRITTEN AND ORAL COMMUNICATION SKILLS.
(Percentage Agreeing)

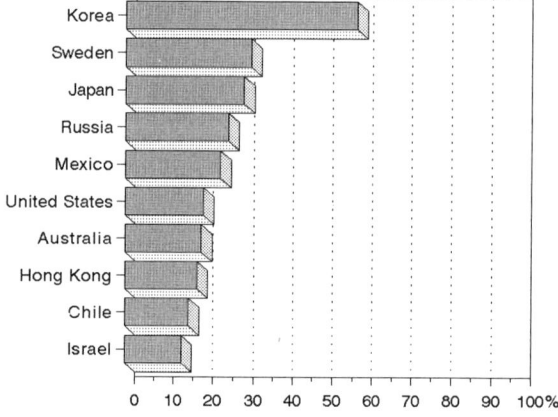

Figure 13
THE UNDERGRADUATES YOU TEACH AT THIS INSTITUTION
ARE ADEQUATELY PREPARED IN MATHEMATICS AND
QUANTITATIVE REASONING SKILLS.
(Percentage Agreeing)

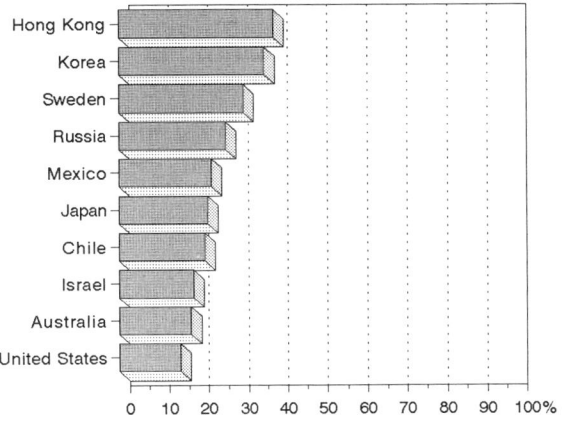

Figure 14
HOW WOULD YOU RATE THE QUALITY OF THE STUDENTS
CURRENTLY ENROLLED IN YOUR DEPARTMENT?
(Percentage Responding "Excellent" or "Good")

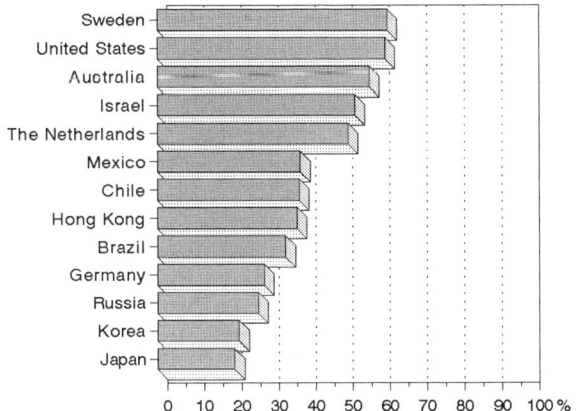

Figure 15
PLEASE INDICATE THE DEGREE TO WHICH YOUR AFFILIATION WITH YOUR ACADEMIC DISCIPLINE IS IMPORTANT TO YOU.
(Percentage Responding "Very Important")

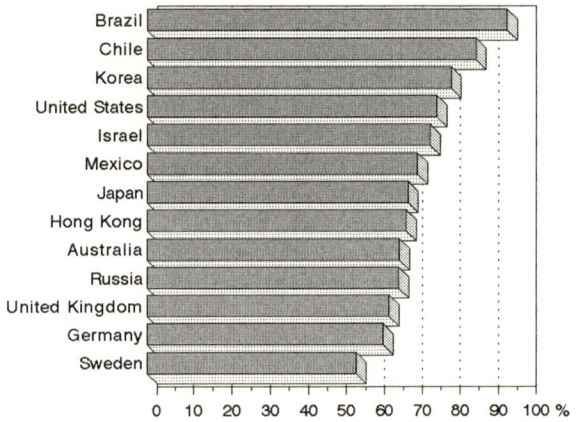

Figure 16
PLEASE INDICATE THE DEGREE TO WHICH YOUR AFFILIATION WITH THIS INSTITUTION IS IMPORTANT TO YOU.
(Percentage Responding "Very Important")

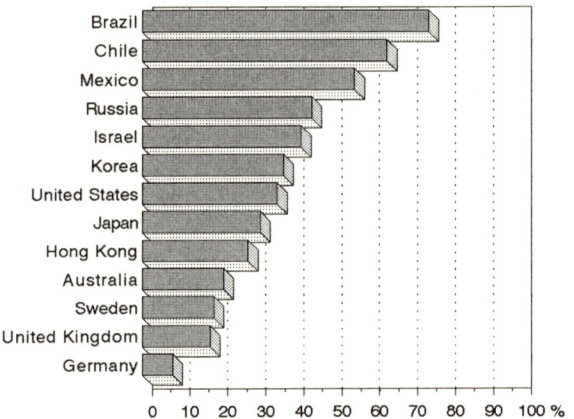

Figure 17
REGARDING YOUR OWN PREFERENCES, DO YOUR INTERESTS LIE PRIMARILY IN TEACHING OR IN RESEARCH?

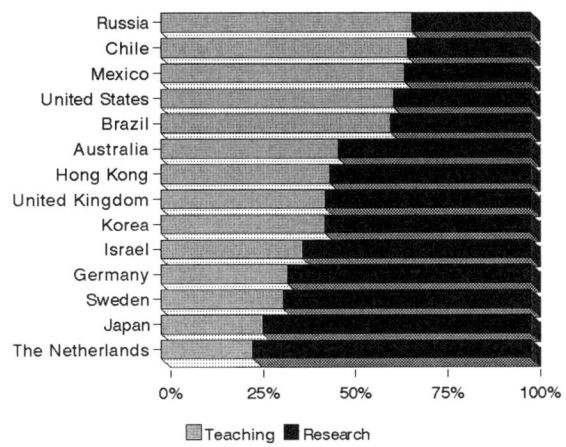

Figure 18
THE PRESSURE TO PUBLISH REDUCES THE QUALITY OF TEACHING AT THIS INSTITUTION.
(Percentage Agreeing)

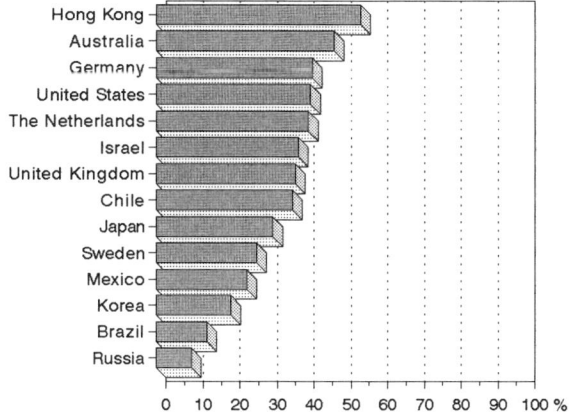

Figure 19
HAVE YOU OR YOUR RESEARCH GROUP RECEIVED ANY GRANTS OR SPECIAL FUNDING IN THE LAST THREE YEARS?
(Percentage Responding "Yes")

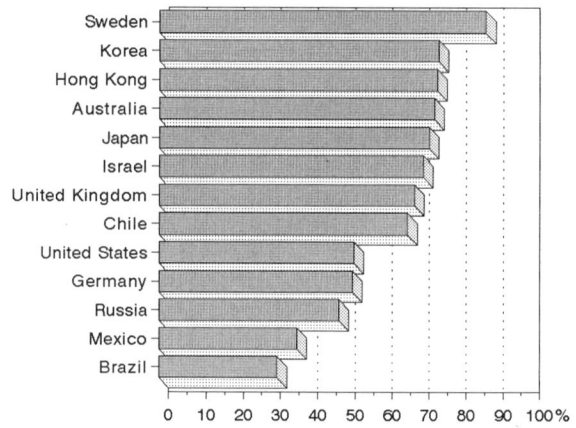

Figure 20
PLEASE ESTIMATE THE TOTAL AMOUNT OF RESEARCH FUNDING YOU OR YOUR RESEARCH GROUP RECEIVED IN THE LAST THREE YEARS.

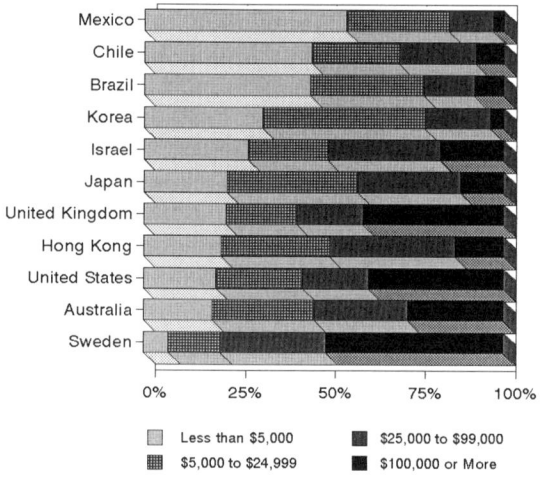

Figure 21
RESEARCH FUNDING IN MY FIELD IS EASIER TO GET NOW
THAN IT WAS FIVE YEARS AGO.
(Percentage Agreeing)

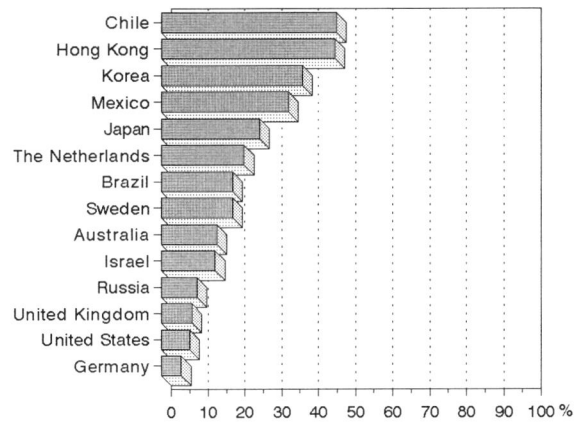

Figure 22
A STRONG RECORD OF SUCCESSFUL RESEARCH ACTIVITY IS
IMPORTANT IN FACULTY EVALUATION AT THIS INSTITUTION.
(Percentage Agreeing)

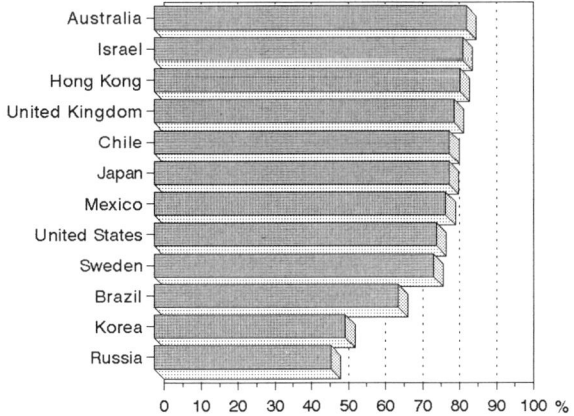

Figure 23
IN MY DEPARTMENT, IT IS DIFFICULT FOR A PERSON TO
ACHIEVE TENURE IF HE OR SHE DOES NOT PUBLISH.
(Percentage Agreeing)

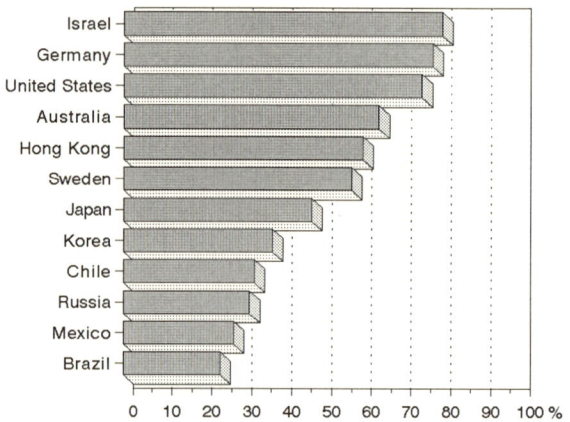

Figure 24
I FREQUENTLY FEEL UNDER PRESSURE TO DO MORE
RESEARCH THAN I ACTUALLY WOULD LIKE TO DO.
(Percentage Agreeing)

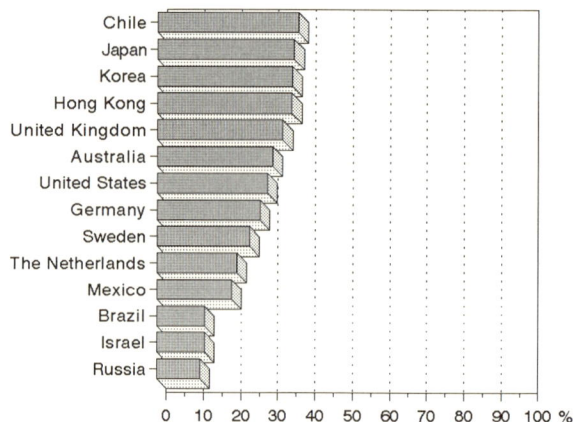

Figure 25

IS YOUR TEACHING REGULARLY EVALUATED?
(Percentage Agreeing)

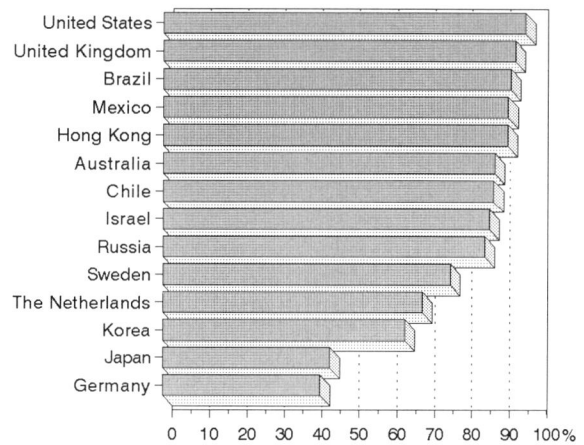

Figure 26

IS YOUR RESEARCH REGULARLY EVALUATED?
(Percentage Agreeing)

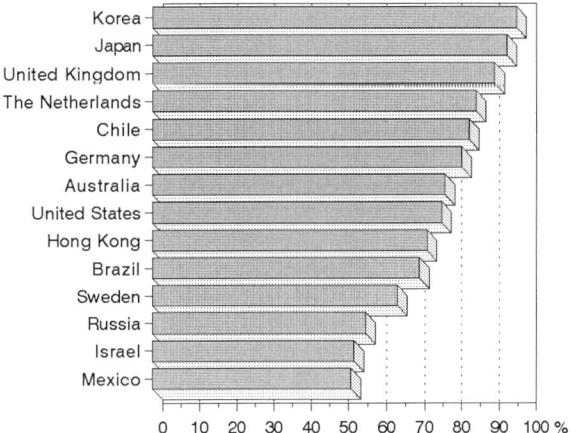

Figure 27
ARE YOUR SERVICE ACTIVITIES REGULARLY EVALUATED?
(Percentage Agreeing)

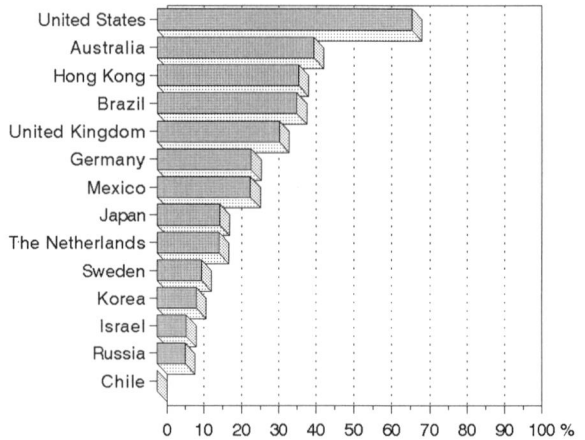

Figure 28
STUDENT OPINIONS SHOULD BE USED IN EVALUATING
THE TEACHING EFFECTIVENESS OF FACULTY.
(Percentage Agreeing)

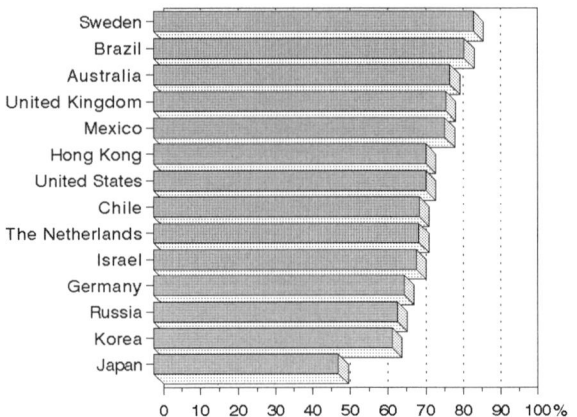

Figure 29

IS YOUR TEACHING REGULARLY EVALUATED BY YOUR STUDENTS?
(Percentage Agreeing)

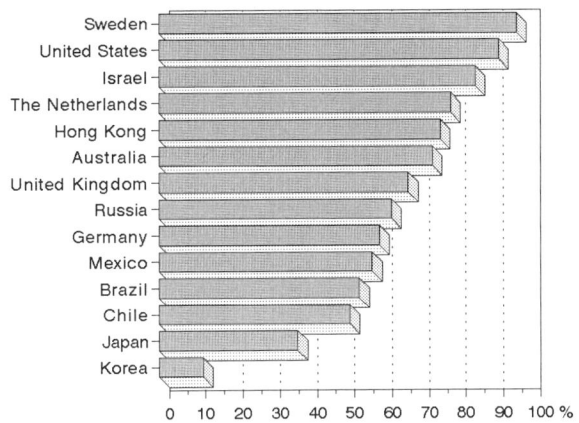

Figure 30

AT THIS INSTITUTION, WE NEED BETTER WAYS TO EVALUATE TEACHING PERFORMANCE.
(Percentage Agreeing)

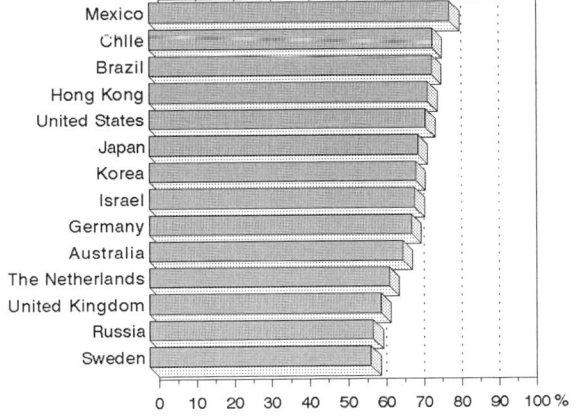

Figure 31

AT THIS INSTITUTION, PUBLICATIONS USED FOR PROMOTION DECISIONS ARE JUST "COUNTED," NOT QUALITATIVELY EVALUATED.
(Percentage Agreeing)

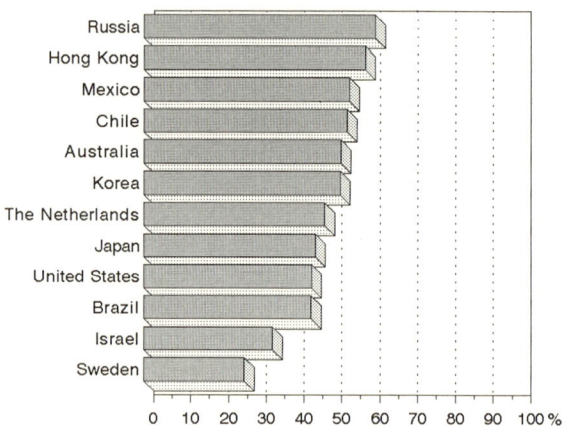

Figure 32

HOW WOULD YOU RATE YOUR OWN ACADEMIC SALARY?
(Percentage Responding "Excellent" or "Good")

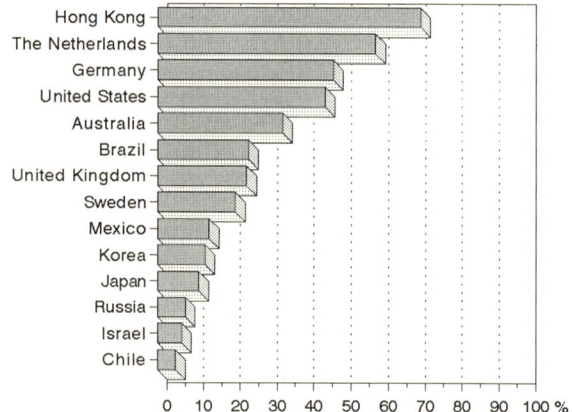

Figure 33
FROM AN ECONOMIC STANDPOINT, IT IS NECESSARY FOR ME
TO ENGAGE IN PAID CONSULTING WORK.
(Percentage Responding "Yes")

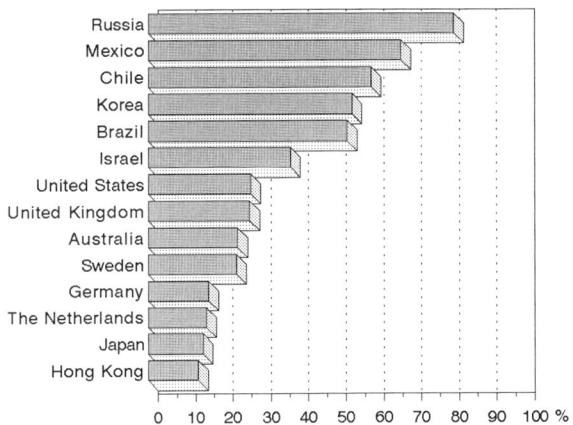

Figure 34
MY JOB IS A SOURCE OF CONSIDERABLE PERSONAL STRAIN.
(Percentage Agreeing)

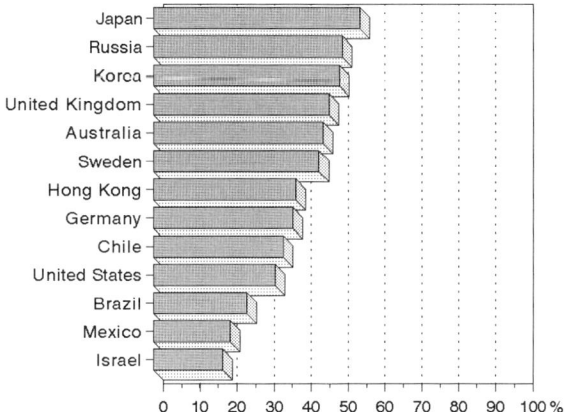

Figure 35
AT THIS INSTITUTION, HOW WOULD YOU EVALUATE THE TECHNOLOGY FOR TEACHING?
(Percentage Responding "Excellent" or "Good")

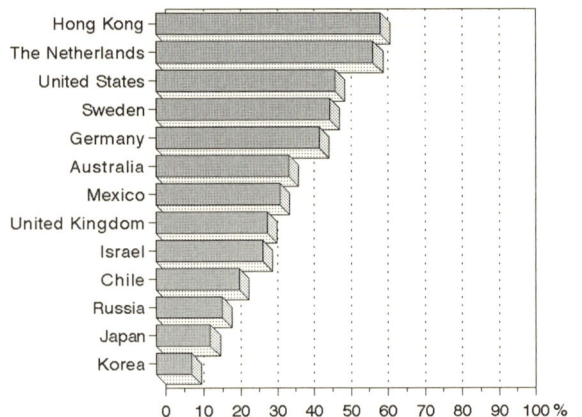

Figure 36
AT THIS INSTITUTION, HOW WOULD YOU EVALUATE THE RESEARCH EQUIPMENT AND INSTRUMENTS?
(Percentage Responding "Excellent" or "Good")

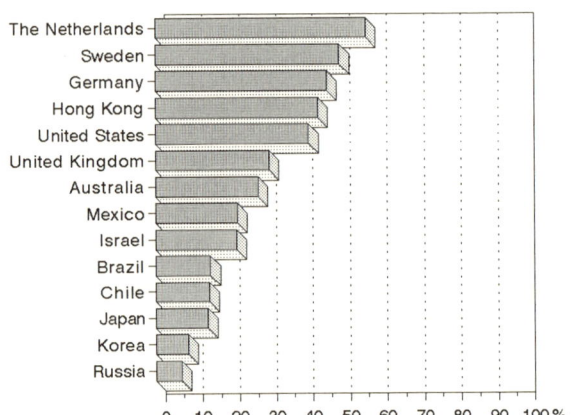

Figure 37
AT THIS INSTITUTION, HOW WOULD YOU EVALUATE THE COMPUTER FACILITIES?
(Percentage Responding "Excellent" or "Good")

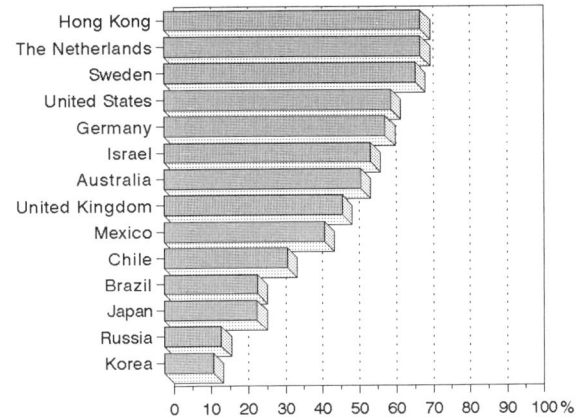

Figure 38
AT THIS INSTITUTION, HOW WOULD YOU EVALUATE THE LIBRARY HOLDINGS?
(Percentage Responding "Excellent" or "Good")

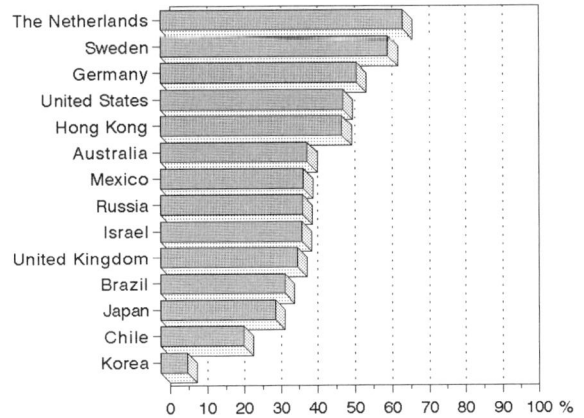

Figure 39
THIS IS AN ESPECIALLY CREATIVE AND PRODUCTIVE TIME IN MY FIELD.
(Percentage Agreeing)

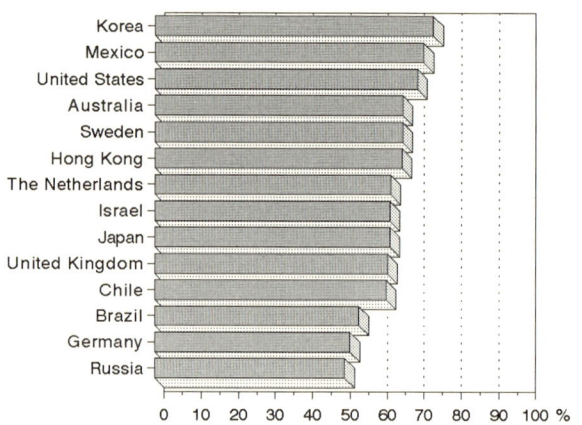

Figure 40
TO WHAT EXTENT ARE YOU SATISFIED WITH THE COURSES YOU TEACH?
(Percentage Responding "Satisfied")

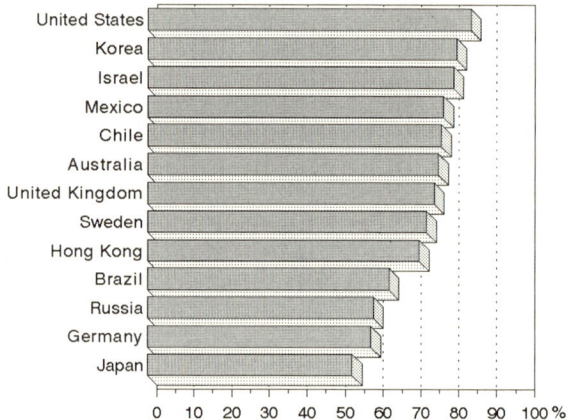

Figure 41

TO WHAT EXTENT ARE YOU SATISFIED WITH THE OPPORTUNITY TO PURSUE YOUR OWN IDEAS?
(Percentage Responding "Satisfied")

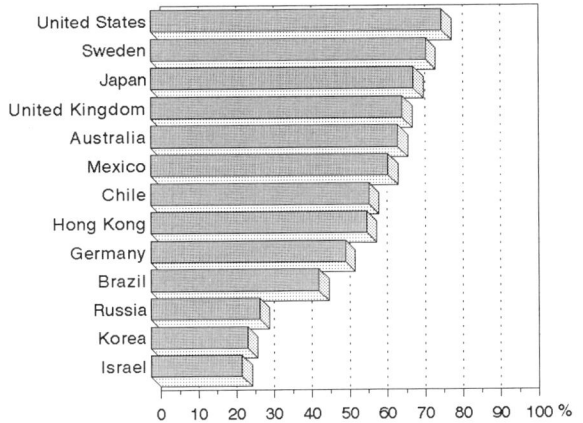

Figure 42

TO WHAT EXTEND ARE YOU SATISFIED WITH YOUR RELATIONSHIPS WITH COLLEAGUES?
(Percentage Responding "Satisfied")

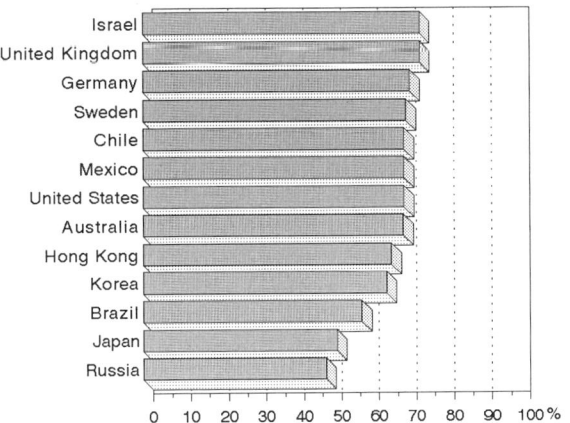

Figure 43
BASED ON YOUR EXPERIENCE AT THIS INSTITUTION, HOW WOULD YOU ASSESS THE INTELLECTUAL ATMOSPHERE?
(Percentage Responding "Excellent" or "Good")

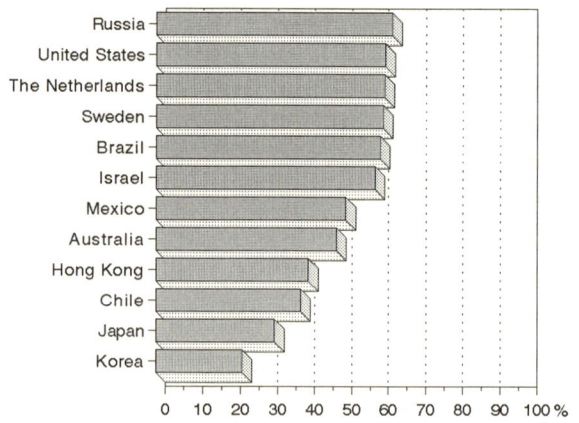

Figure 44
THIS IS A POOR TIME FOR ANY YOUNG PERSON TO BEGIN AN ACADEMIC CAREER IN MY FIELD.
(Percentage Agreeing)

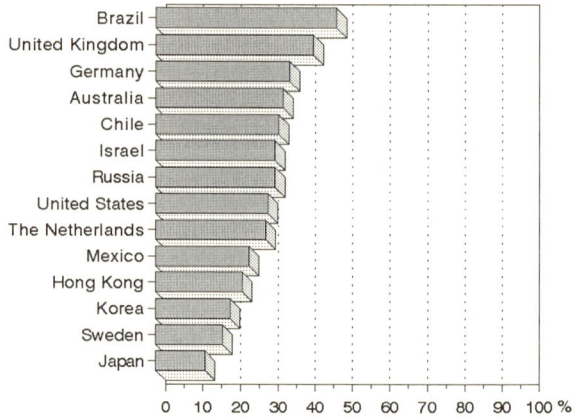

Figure 45
IF I HAD IT TO DO OVER AGAIN, I WOULD NOT BECOME
AN ACADEMIC.
(Percentage Agreeing)

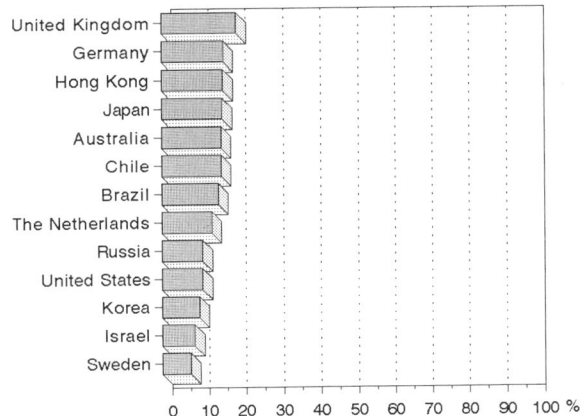

Figure 46
HOW INFLUENTIAL ARE YOU, PERSONALLY, IN HELPING
TO SHAPE KEY ACADEMIC POLICIES
AT THE INSTITUTIONAL LEVEL?
(Percentage Responding "Not at All Influential")

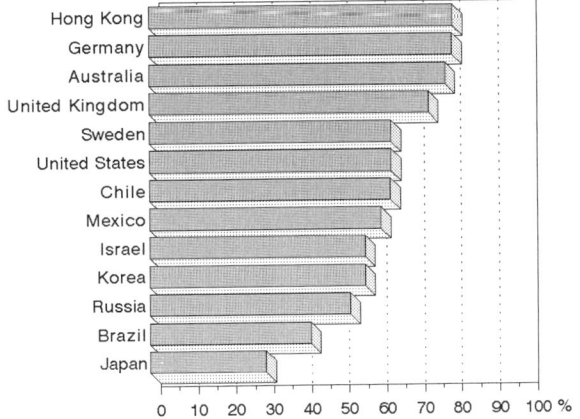

Figure 47
BASED ON YOUR EXPERIENCE AT THIS INSTITUTION,
HOW WOULD YOU ASSESS RELATIONSHIPS
BETWEEN FACULTY AND ADMINISTRATION?
(Percentage Responding "Fair" or "Poor")

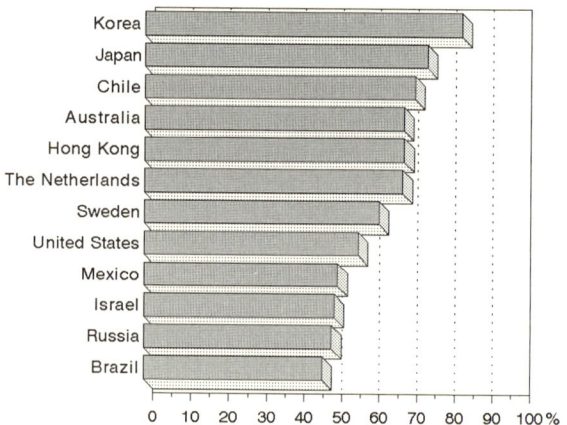

Figure 48
I AM KEPT INFORMED ABOUT WHAT IS GOING ON
AT THIS INSTITUTION.
(Percentage Agreeing)

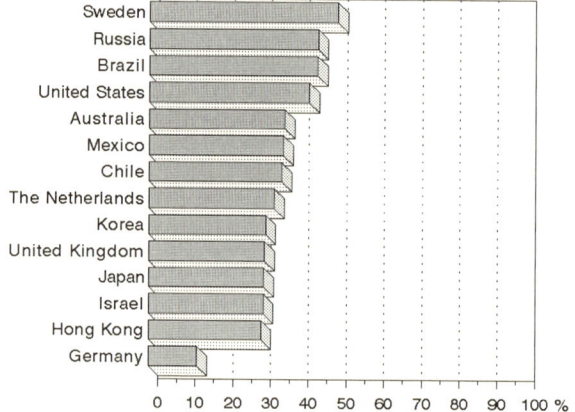

Figure 49

COMMUNICATION BETWEEN THE FACULTY AND
THE ADMINISTRATION IS POOR.
(Percentage Agreeing)

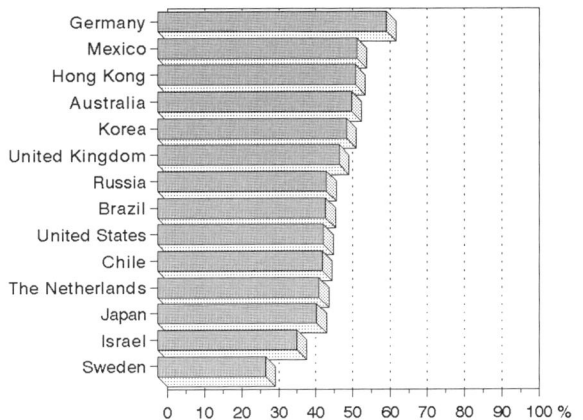

Figure 50

THE ADMINISTRATION IS OFTEN AUTOCRATIC.
(Percentage Agreeing)

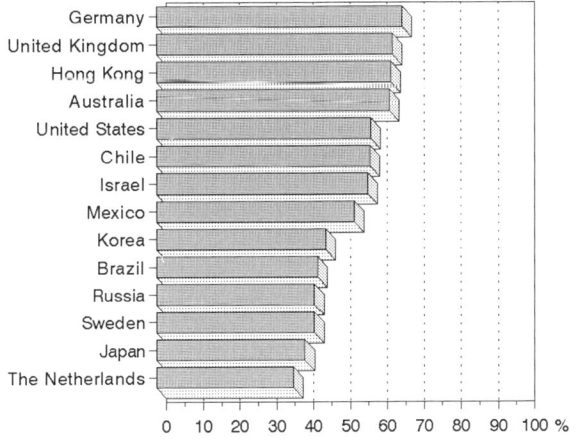

Figure 51
LACK OF FACULTY INVOLVEMENT IS A REAL PROBLEM.
(Percentage Agreeing)

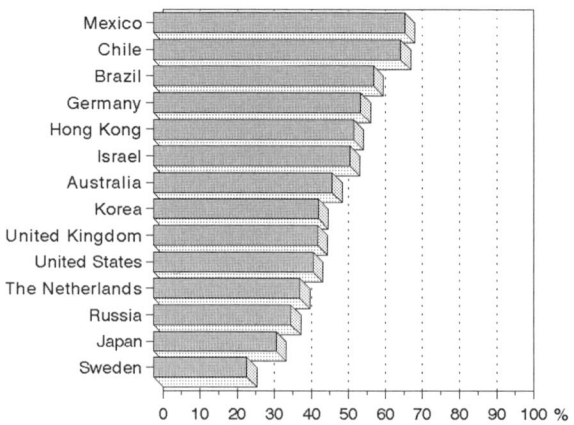

Figure 52
TOP-LEVEL ADMINISTRATORS ARE PROVIDING COMPETENT LEADERSHIP.
(Percentage Agreeing)

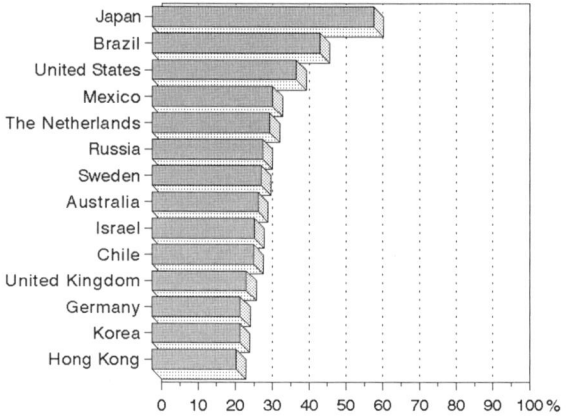

Figure 53
THE ADMINISTRATION SUPPORTS ACADEMIC FREEDOM.
(Percentage Agreeing)

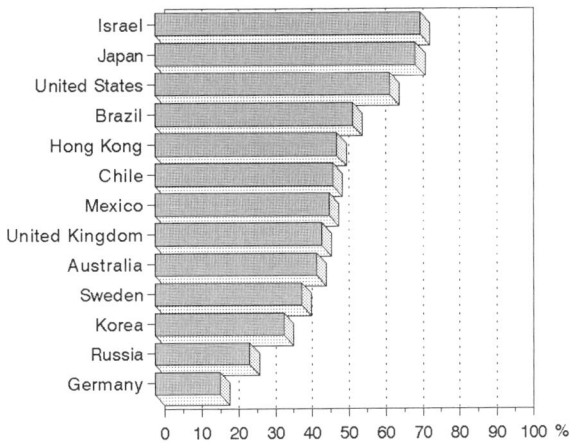

Figure 54
THE GOVERNMENT SHOULD HAVE THE RESPONSIBILITY TO DEFINE THE OVERALL PURPOSES AND POLICIES FOR HIGHER EDUCATION.
(Percentage Agreeing)

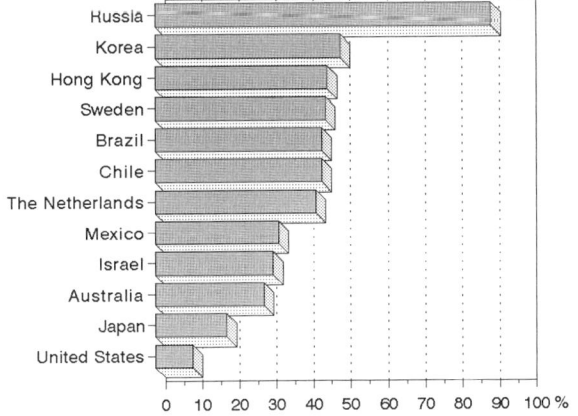

Figure 55

IN THIS COUNTRY, THERE IS FAR TOO MUCH GOVERNMENTAL INTERFERENCE IN IMPORTANT ACADEMIC POLICIES.
(Percentage Agreeing)

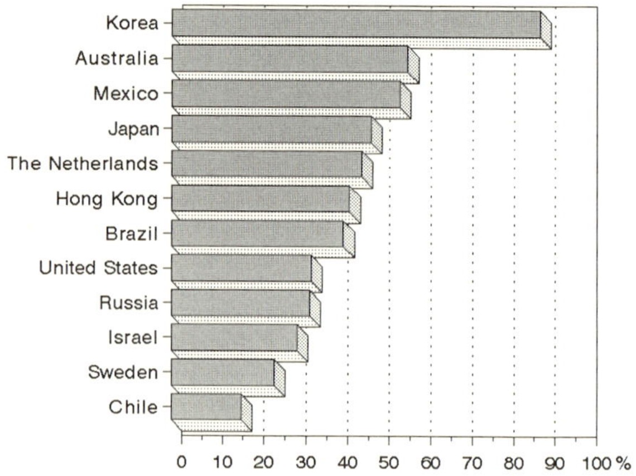

Figure 56

IS ACADEMIC FREEDOM STRONGLY PROTECTED IN THIS COUNTRY?
(Percentage Responding "Yes")

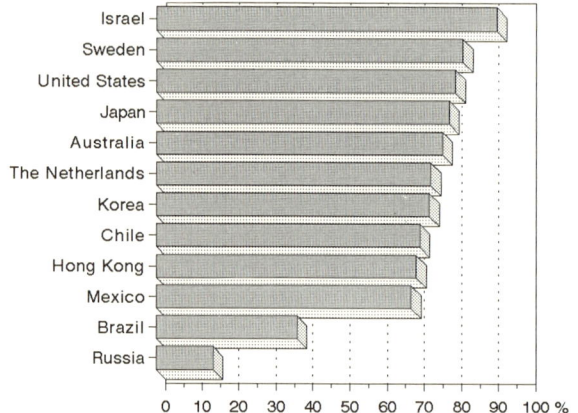

Figure 57

**I CAN FOCUS MY RESEARCH ON ANY TOPIC
OF SPECIAL INTEREST TO ME.**
(Percentage Agreeing)

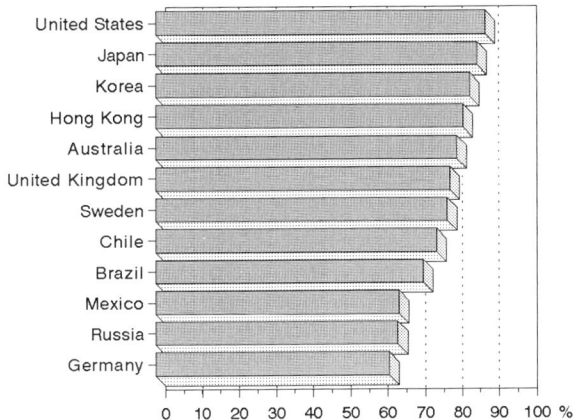

Figure 58

**AT THIS INSTITUTION, I AM FULLY FREE TO DETERMINE
THE CONTENT OF THE COURSES I TEACH.**
(Percentage Agreeing)

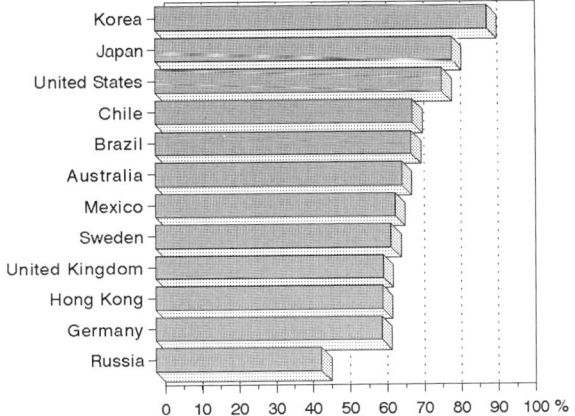

Figure 59

IN THIS COUNTRY, THERE ARE NO POLITICAL OR IDEOLOGICAL RESTRICTIONS ON WHAT A SCHOLAR MAY PUBLISH.
(Percentage Disagreeing)

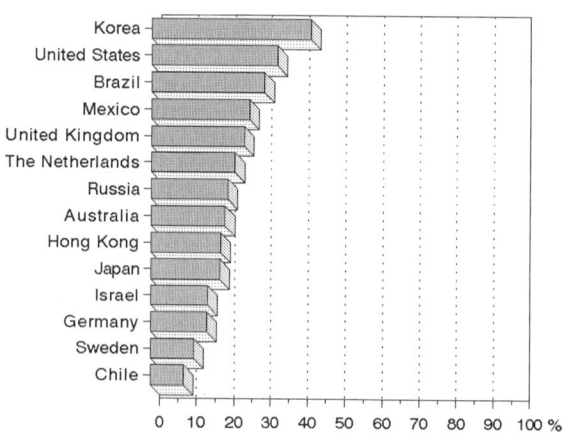

Figure 60

RESPECT FOR ACADEMICS IS DECLINING.
(Percentage Agreeing)

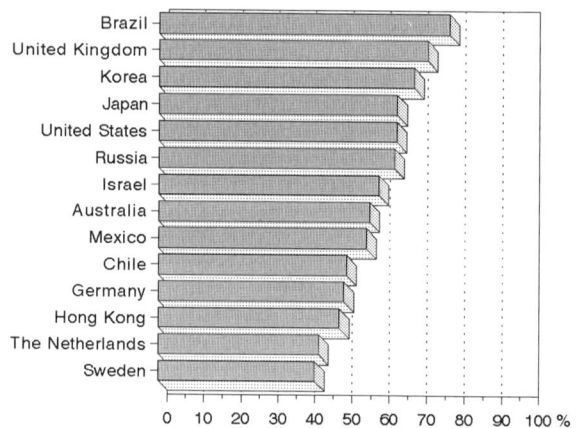

Figure 61
ACADEMICS ARE AMONG THE MOST INFLUENTIAL OPINION LEADERS IN MY COUNTRY.
(Percentage Agreeing)

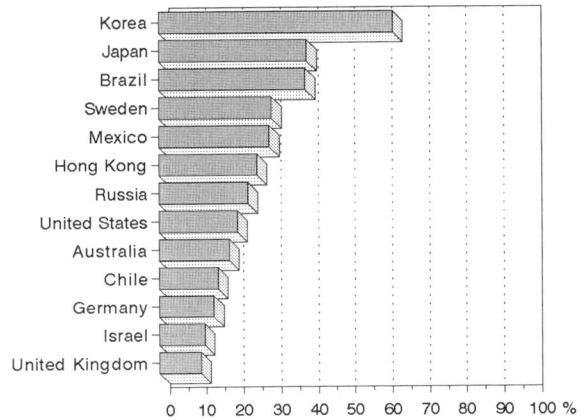

Figure 62
FACULTY IN MY DISCIPLINE HAVE A PROFESSIONAL OBLIGATION TO APPLY THEIR KNOWLEDGE TO PROBLEMS IN SOCIETY.
(Percentage Responding "Yes")

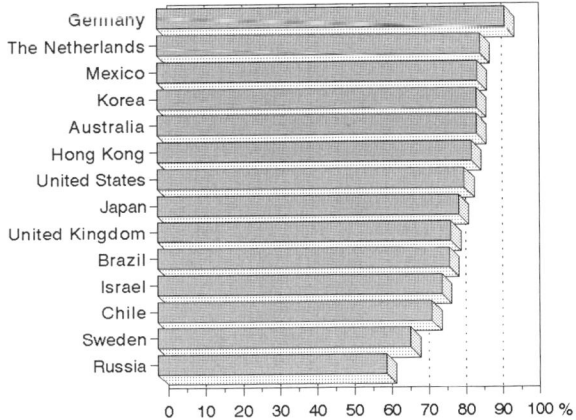

Figure 63
DURING THE PAST THREE YEARS AT THIS INSTITUTION,
HOW FREQUENTLY HAVE FOREIGN STUDENTS
BEEN ENROLLED?
(Percentage Responding "Frequently" or "Occasionally")

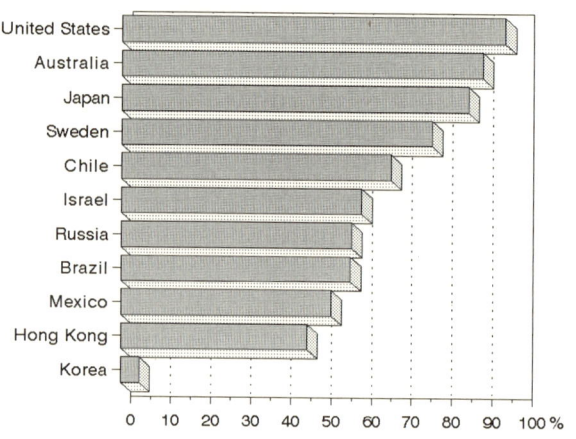

Figure 64
DURING THE PAST THREE YEARS AT THIS INSTITUTION,
HOW FREQUENTLY HAVE YOUR STUDENTS STUDIED ABROAD?
(Percentage Responding "Frequently" or "Occasionally")

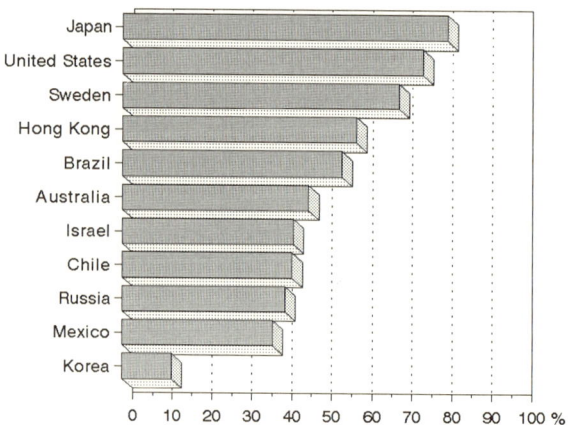

Figure 65
THE CURRICULUM AT THIS INSTITUTION SHOULD BE MORE INTERNATIONAL IN FOCUS.
(Percentage Agreeing)

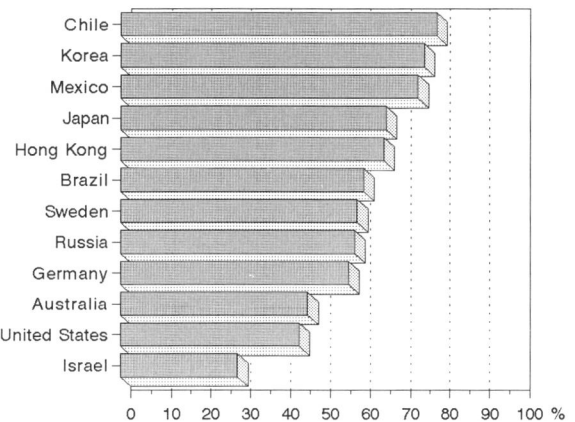

Figure 66
FOR HOW MANY MONTHS DURING THE PAST THREE YEARS, HAVE YOU TRAVELLED ABROAD TO STUDY OR DO RESEARCH?

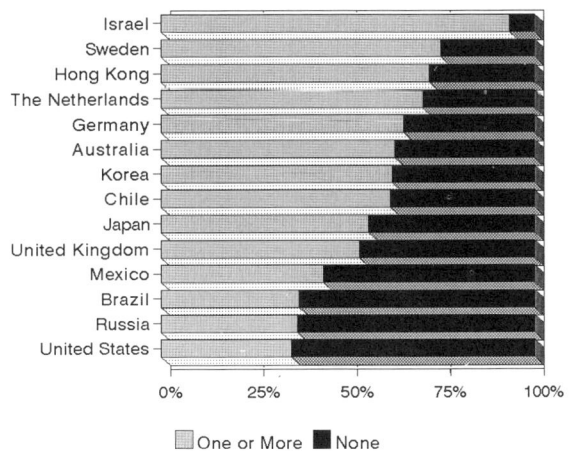

Figure 67
FOR HOW MANY MONTHS DURING THE PAST THREE YEARS,
HAVE YOU SERVED AS A FACULTY MEMBER AT
AN INSTITUTION IN ANOTHER COUNTRY?

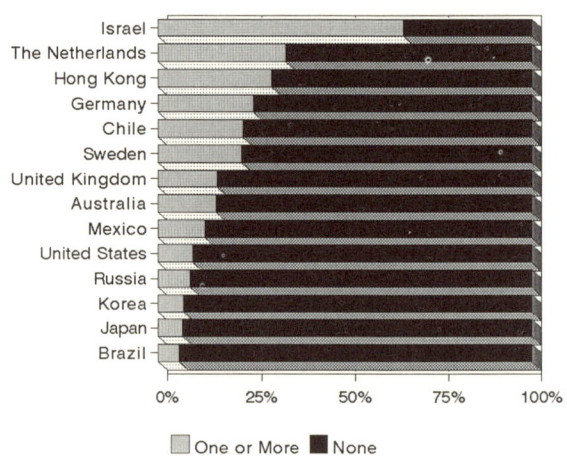

Figure 68
IN ORDER TO KEEP UP WITH DEVELOPMENTS IN MY
DISCIPLINE, A SCHOLAR MUST READ BOOKS AND JOURNALS
PUBLISHED ABROAD.
(Percentage Agreeing)

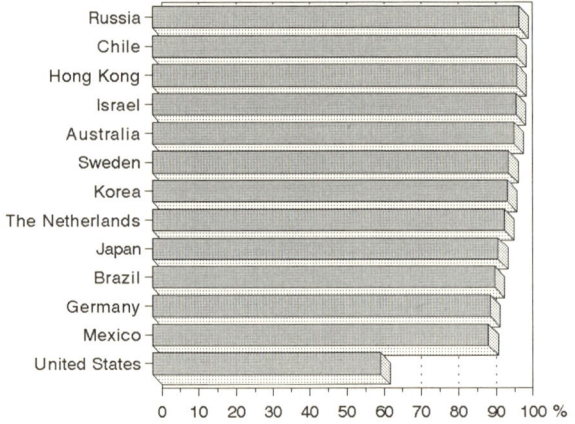

Figure 69
CONNECTIONS WITH SCHOLARS IN OTHER COUNTRIES ARE
VERY IMPORTANT TO MY PROFESSIONAL WORK.
(Percentage Agreeing)

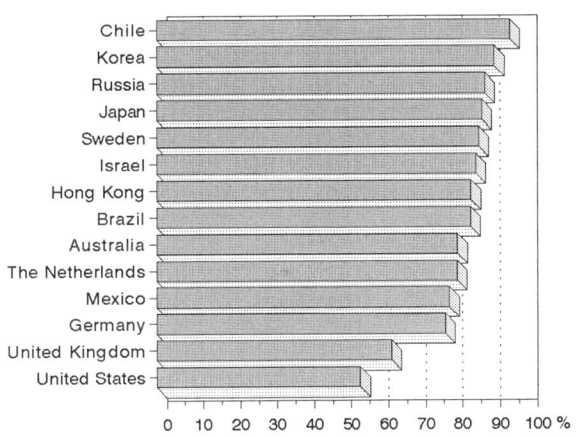

Figure 70
A SCHOLAR'S INTERNATIONAL CONNECTIONS ARE
IMPORTANT IN FACULTY EVALUATION AT THIS INSTITUTION.
(Percentage Agreeing)

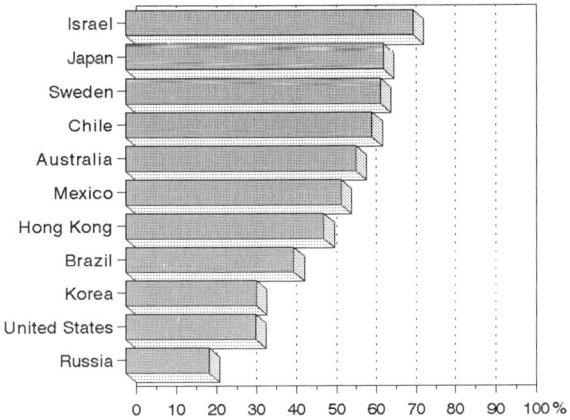

TABLES

Table 1

	WHAT IS YOUR GENDER?	
	FEMALE	MALE
Australia	35%	65%
Brazil	39	61
Chile	33	67
Germany	17	83
Hong Kong	25	75
Israel	28	72
Japan	8	92
Korea	13	87
Mexico	36	64
The Netherlands	22	78
Russia	26	74
Sweden	26	74
United Kingdom	23	77
United States	30	70

Table 2

	HOW OLD ARE YOU?
	MEAN AGE
Australia	45
Brazil	43
Chile	47
Germany	41
Hong Kong	42
Israel	51
Japan	51
Korea	45
Mexico	39
The Netherlands	42
Russia	51
Sweden	47
United Kingdom	45
United States	48

Table 3

AT HOW MANY DIFFERENT INSTITUTIONS OF HIGHER EDUCATION HAVE YOU EVER HELD A REGULAR ACADEMIC APPOINTMENT?

	ONE OR TWO	THREE OR MORE
Australia	68%	32%
Brazil	70	30
Chile	80	20
Germany	80	20
Hong Kong	75	25
Israel	74	26
Japan	89	11
Korea	95	5
Mexico	88	12
The Netherlands	88	12
Russia	91	9
Sweden	79	21
United Kingdom	78	22
United States	75	25

Table 4

IS YOUR CURRENT EMPLOYMENT AT THIS INSTITUTION FULL TIME OR PART TIME?

	FULL TIME	PART TIME
Australia	95%	5%
Brazil	56	44
Chile	78	22
Germany	82	18
Hong Kong	99	1
Israel	81	19
Japan	99	1
Korea	100	0
Mexico	62	38
Russia	95	5
Sweden	82	18
United Kingdom	94	6
United States	89	11

Table 5

DO YOU CURRENTLY HOLD OTHER PAID ACADEMIC POSITIONS OUTSIDE THIS INSTITUTION?

	YES, FULL TIME	YES, PART TIME	NO
Australia	0%	4%	96%
Brazil	24	2	74
Chile	5	31	64
Germany	1	12	87
Hong Kong	0	11	89
Israel	4	33	63
Japan	1	35	64
Korea	5	6	89
Mexico	5	22	73
The Netherlands	6	1	93
Sweden	2	15	83
United Kingdom	0	8	91
United States	2	8	90

Table 6

DO YOU CURRENTLY HOLD OTHER PAID NONACADEMIC POSITIONS OUTSIDE THIS INSTITUTION?

	YES, FULL TIME	YES, PART TIME	NO
Australia	0%	9%	91%
Brazil	33	14	54
Chile	5	29	67
Germany	1	11	88
Hong Kong	0	5	95
Israel	5	16	80
Japan	2	17	82
Korea	4	3	92
Mexico	15	26	60
The Netherlands	11	1	88
Sweden	2	20	78
United Kingdom	1	6	93
United States	3	16	81

Table 7

OF YOUR TOTAL EARNED INCOME, WHAT PERCENTAGE COMES FROM THIS INSTITUTION?

	PERCENTAGE
Australia	95%
Brazil	64
Chile	78
Germany	94
Hong Kong	97
Israel	84
Japan	90
Korea	90
Mexico	72
The Netherlands	89
Russia	83
Sweden	85
United Kingdom	94
United States	87

Table 8

IN YOUR OPINION, WHAT PERCENTAGE OF THE YOUNG PEOPLE IN YOUR COUNTRY ARE CAPABLE OF COMPLETING SECONDARY EDUCATION?

	PERCENTAGE
Australia	79%
Brazil	22
Chile	64
Germany	36
Hong Kong	77
Israel	73
Japan	75
Korea	70
Mexico	55
Russia	69
Sweden	76
United States	79

Table 9

IN YOUR OPINION, WHAT PERCENTAGE OF STUDENTS IN
YOUR COUNTRY WHO COMPLETE SECONDARY EDUCATION
SHOULD BE ADMITTED TO HIGHER EDUCATION?

	PERCENTAGE
Australia	49%
Brazil	51
Chile	38
Germany	73
Hong Kong	50
Israel	61
Japan	55
Korea	44
Mexico	62
Russia	31
Sweden	54
United States	61

Table 10

ACCESS TO HIGHER EDUCATION SHOULD BE AVAILABLE
TO ALL WHO MEET MINIMUM ENTRANCE REQUIREMENTS.

	AGREE	NEUTRAL	DISAGREE
Australia	75%	9%	16%
Brazil	70	6	25
Chile	66	14	20
Germany	61	12	28
Hong Kong	71	12	17
Israel	82	7	11
Japan	55	21	24
Korea	64	13	23
Mexico	74	9	18
The Netherlands	43	13	44
Russia	61	12	28
Sweden	69	15	16
United Kingdom	87	6	7
United States	79	7	14

Table 11
ADMISSION STANDARDS SHOULD BE LOWERED TO PERMIT DISADVANTAGED STUDENTS TO ENROLL AT THIS INSTITUTION.

	AGREE	NEUTRAL	DISAGREE
Australia	54%	26%	20%
Brazil	17	12	71
Chile	38	13	49
Germany	30	17	53
Hong Kong	19	21	60
Israel	22	15	63
Japan	9	27	64
Mexico	15	11	74
Russia	12	17	72
Sweden	7	17	76
United States	17	13	70

Table 12
THE UNDERGRADUATES YOU TEACH AT THIS INSTITUTION ARE ADEQUATELY PREPARED IN WRITTEN AND ORAL COMMUNICATION SKILLS.

	AGREE	NEUTRAL	DISAGREE
Australia	20%	15%	65%
Chile	17	21	62
Hong Kong	19	15	66
Israel	15	27	59
Japan	30	27	42
Korea	59	24	17
Mexico	24	18	58
Russia	26	37	37
Sweden	32	24	44
United States	20	17	63

Table 13

THE UNDERGRADUATES YOU TEACH AT THIS INSTITUTION ARE ADEQUATELY PREPARED IN MATHEMATICS AND QUANTITATIVE REASONING SKILLS.

	AGREE	NEUTRAL	DISAGREE
Australia	18%	27%	55%
Chile	22	29	49
Hong Kong	39	27	34
Israel	19	24	57
Japan	22	33	44
Korea	37	33	31
Mexico	23	19	58
Russia	27	37	36
Sweden	32	32	36
United States	15	21	64

Table 14

HOW WOULD YOU RATE THE QUALITY OF THE STUDENTS CURRENTLY ENROLLED IN YOUR DEPARTMENT?

	EXCELLENT	GOOD	FAIR	POOR
Australia	10%	47%	37%	6%
Brazil	2	32	55	11
Chile	3	35	49	12
Germany	2	27	55	16
Hong Kong	2	36	52	10
Israel	8	45	39	7
Japan	3	18	51	29
Korea	4	18	40	38
Mexico	3	36	49	13
The Netherlands	10	51	45	4
Russia	1	27	62	11
Sweden	6	56	35	3
United States	11	50	34	5

Table 15

PLEASE INDICATE THE DEGREE TO WHICH YOUR AFFILIATION WITH YOUR ACADEMIC DISCIPLINE IS IMPORTANT TO YOU.

	VERY IMPORTANT	FAIRLY IMPORTANT	NOT TOO IMPORTANT	NOT AT ALL IMPORTANT
Australia	67%	27%	5%	2%
Brazil	95	4	1	0
Chile	87	13	0	0
Germany	62	29	6	3
Hong Kong	68	27	3	2
Israel	75	23	2	0
Japan	69	28	3	0
Korea	80	19	1	0
Mexico	71	26	2	0
Russia	66	30	3	1
Sweden	55	34	9	2
United Kingdom	64	29	6	1
United States	77	21	3	0

Table 16

PLEASE INDICATE THE DEGREE TO WHICH YOUR AFFILIATION WITH THIS INSTITUTION IS IMPORTANT TO YOU.

	VERY IMPORTANT	FAIRLY IMPORTANT	NOT TOO IMPORTANT	NOT AT ALL IMPORTANT
Australia	22%	52%	21%	6%
Brazil	76	19	5	1
Chile	65	30	5	1
Germany	8	26	35	31
Hong Kong	28	50	18	4
Israel	42	46	10	2
Japan	31	48	19	2
Korea	37	51	11	1
Mexico	56	38	6	0
Russia	45	45	10	1
Sweden	19	47	29	5
United Kingdom	18	46	28	8
United States	36	46	15	3

Table 17

REGARDING YOUR OWN PREFERENCES, DO YOUR INTERESTS LIE PRIMARILY IN TEACHING OR IN RESEARCH?

	PRIMARILY IN TEACHING	LEANING TO TEACHING	LEANING TO RESEARCH	PRIMARILY IN RESEARCH
Australia	13%	35%	43%	9%
Brazil	20	42	36	3
Chile	18	49	28	5
Germany	8	27	47	19
Hong Kong	11	35	46	8
Israel	11	27	48	14
Japan	4	24	55	17
Korea	5	40	50	6
Mexico	22	43	31	4
The Netherlands	7	18	46	30
Russia	18	50	29	3
Sweden	12	21	44	23
United Kingdom	12	32	40	15
United States	27	36	30	7

Table 18

THE PRESSURE TO PUBLISH REDUCES THE QUALITY OF TEACHING AT THIS INSTITUTION.

	AGREE	NEUTRAL	DISAGREE
Australia	48%	23%	29%
Brazil	14	23	63
Chile	37	28	36
Germany	42	18	40
Hong Kong	55	18	27
Israel	38	12	50
Japan	31	40	29
Korea	20	36	44
Mexico	24	34	42
The Netherlands	41	22	37
Russia	9	38	53
Sweden	27	24	49
United Kingdom	38	25	37
United States	42	18	41

Table 19

HAVE YOU OR YOUR RESEARCH GROUP RECEIVED ANY
GRANTS OR SPECIAL FUNDING IN THE LAST THREE YEARS?

	YES	NO
Australia	74%	26%
Brazil	32	68
Chile	67	33
Germany	52	48
Hong Kong	75	25
Israel	71	29
Japan	73	27
Korea	75	25
Mexico	37	63
Russia	48	52
Sweden	88	12
United Kingdom	69	31
United States	52	48

Table 20

PLEASE ESTIMATE THE TOTAL AMOUNT OF RESEARCH
FUNDING YOU OR YOUR RESEARCH GROUP RECEIVED
IN THE LAST THREE YEARS.

	LESS THAN $5,000	$5,000 TO $24,999	$25,000 TO $49,999	$50,000 TO $99,999	$100,000 TO $249,999	$250,000 TO $499,999	$500,000 OR MORE
Australia	19%	28%	14%	13%	16%	5%	6%
Brazil	46	32	9	5	5	1	2
Chile	47	24	13	9	5	2	1
Hong Kong	21	30	18	17	11	1	1
Israel	29	22	19	12	13	4	1
Japan	23	36	16	13	9	2	2
Korea	33	45	12	6	3	1	0
Mexico	56	28	9	4	2	2	0
Sweden	7	15	10	19	21	15	14
United Kingdom	23	20	7	11	16	10	13
United States	20	24	9	10	15	11	12

Table 21

RESEARCH FUNDING IN MY FIELD IS EASIER TO GET NOW THAN IT WAS FIVE YEARS AGO.

	AGREE	NEUTRAL	DISAGREE
Australia	15%	23%	62%
Brazil	19	21	60
Chile	47	25	27
Germany	5	11	83
Hong Kong	47	28	25
Israel	15	17	68
Japan	27	49	25
Korea	38	22	39
Mexico	35	24	42
The Netherlands	23	28	50
Russia	10	13	77
Sweden	19	34	47
United Kingdom	8	25	67
United States	8	21	71

Table 22

A STRONG RECORD OF SUCCESSFUL RESEARCH ACTIVITY IS IMPORTANT IN FACULTY EVALUATION AT THIS INSTITUTION.

	AGREE	NEUTRAL	DISAGREE
Australia	85%	8%	7%
Brazil	66	14	20
Chile	80	13	8
Hong Kong	83	9	8
Israel	84	6	10
Japan	80	14	7
Korea	52	22	27
Mexico	79	14	8
Russia	48	36	17
Sweden	76	14	10
United Kingdom	81	9	10
United States	76	9	14

Table 23

IN MY DEPARTMENT, IT IS DIFFICULT FOR A PERSON TO ACHIEVE TENURE IF HE OR SHE DOES NOT PUBLISH.

	AGREE	NEUTRAL	DISAGREE
Australia	64%	15%	21%
Brazil	25	21	55
Chile	33	35	32
Germany	78	8	14
Hong Kong	60	16	24
Israel	81	4	15
Japan	48	23	29
Korea	38	15	48
Mexico	28	24	48
Russia	32	41	27
Sweden	58	18	24
United States	75	8	17

Table 24

I FREQUENTLY FEEL UNDER PRESSURE TO DO MORE RESEARCH THAN I ACTUALLY WOULD LIKE TO DO.

	AGREE	NEUTRAL	DISAGREE
Australia	31%	23%	46%
Brazil	13	17	71
Chile	38	27	36
Germany	28	17	55
Hong Kong	36	21	43
Israel	13	12	76
Japan	37	31	32
Korea	36	18	45
Mexico	20	25	55
The Netherlands	22	26	52
Russia	12	47	41
Sweden	25	21	54
United Kingdom	34	24	42
United States	30	20	50

Table 25

WHICH OF THESE ACTIVITIES ARE APPRAISED OR EVALUATED REGULARLY?

(More than one response could be selected.)

	TEACHING	RESEARCH	SERVICE
Australia	89%	78%	42%
Brazil	93	71	38
Chile	88	85	0
Germany	42	83	25
Hong Kong	92	73	38
Israel	87	54	8
Japan	45	95	17
Korea	65	97	11
Mexico	92	53	25
The Netherlands	69	87	17
Russia	86	57	8
Sweden	77	65	12
United Kingdom	94	91	33
United States	97	77	68

Table 26

STUDENT OPINIONS SHOULD BE USED IN EVALUATING THE TEACHING EFFECTIVENESS OF FACULTY.

	AGREE	NEUTRAL	DISAGREE
Australia	79%	11%	10%
Brazil	83	8	9
Chile	71	17	12
Germany	67	17	16
Hong Kong	73	13	14
Israel	70	16	14
Japan	50	28	23
Korea	64	21	15
Mexico	78	13	9
The Netherlands	71	18	12
Russia	65	24	11
Sweden	86	9	6
United Kingdom	78	12	10
United States	73	12	15

Table 27

BY WHOM IS YOUR TEACHING REGULARLY EVALUATED?
(More than one response could be selected.)

	YOUR PEERS IN YOUR DEPARTMENT	THE HEAD OF YOUR DEPARTMENT	MEMBERS OF OTHER DEPARTMENTS AT THIS INSTITUTION	SENIOR ADMINISTRATIVE STAFF AT THIS INSTITUTION	YOUR STUDENTS	EXTERNAL REVIEWERS
Australia	28%	64%	6%	11%	74%	6%
Brazil	53	51	15	28	54	5
Chile	30	61	26	23	51	4
Germany	30	44	6	8	59	2
Hong Kong	23	70	7	23	76	24
Israel	24	45	7	7	85	7
Japan	42	43	10	41	37	5
Korea	18	29	9	70	12	8
Mexico	37	62	23	55	57	10
The Netherlands	49	29	7	7	79	17
Russia	32	76	14	21	62	6
Sweden	20	26	11	7	96	9
United Kingdom	16	67	7	13	67	21
United States	49	78	16	34	91	7

Table 28

AT THIS INSTITUTION, WE NEED BETTER WAYS TO EVALUATE TEACHING PERFORMANCE.

	AGREE	NEUTRAL	DISAGREE
Australia	67%	21%	13%
Brazil	75	15	11
Chile	75	18	7
Germany	69	17	14
Hong Kong	74	19	7
Israel	70	12	17
Japan	71	23	6
Korea	71	21	8
Mexico	80	13	8
The Netherlands	63	26	10
Russia	59	35	6
Sweden	59	26	16
United Kingdom	61	24	15
United States	73	16	11

Table 29

AT THIS INSTITUTION, PUBLICATIONS USED
FOR PROMOTION DECISIONS ARE JUST "COUNTED,"
NOT QUALITATIVELY EVALUATED.

	AGREE	NEUTRAL	DISAGREE
Australia	52%	27%	20%
Brazil	45	22	34
Chile	54	24	22
Hong Kong	59	24	18
Israel	34	20	45
Japan	46	28	27
Korea	52	17	31
Mexico	55	21	24
The Netherlands	48	18	34
Russia	61	25	14
Sweden	27	28	45
United States	45	17	38

Table 30

HOW WOULD YOU RATE YOUR OWN ACADEMIC SALARY?

	EXCELLENT	GOOD	FAIR	POOR
Australia	3%	31%	44%	22%
Brazil	3	22	27	48
Chile	0	5	28	67
Germany	7	41	39	13
Hong Kong	25	46	23	5
Israel	1	6	30	64
Japan	1	10	45	44
Korea	1	12	36	51
Mexico	1	14	32	54
The Netherlands	9	50	31	10
Russia	1	7	16	76
Sweden	2	20	41	38
United Kingdom	2	22	47	29
United States	9	37	35	20

Table 31

FROM AN ECONOMIC STANDPOINT, IT IS NECESSARY FOR ME TO ENGAGE IN PAID CONSULTING WORK.

	YES	NO
Australia	24%	76%
Brazil	53	47
Chile	59	41
Germany	16	84
Hong Kong	13	87
Israel	38	62
Japan	15	85
Korea	54	46
Mexico	67	33
The Netherlands	15	85
Russia	81	19
Sweden	24	76
United Kingdom	27	73
United States	27	73

Table 32

MY JOB IS A SOURCE OF CONSIDERABLE PERSONAL STRAIN.

	AGREE	NEUTRAL	DISAGREE
Australia	46%	21%	33%
Brazil	25	14	61
Chile	35	27	38
Germany	38	20	42
Hong Kong	39	27	34
Israel	19	18	64
Japan	56	30	14
Korea	50	19	31
Mexico	21	19	60
Russia	51	34	15
Sweden	45	26	29
United Kingdom	47	21	32
United States	33	20	47

Table 33

AT THIS INSTITUTION, HOW WOULD YOU EVALUATE THE TECHNOLOGY FOR TEACHING?

	EXCELLENT	GOOD	FAIR	POOR
Australia	3%	32%	43%	21%
Chile	2	21	46	32
Germany	6	39	42	14
Hong Kong	13	48	32	8
Israel	5	24	47	24
Japan	1	13	46	40
Korea	1	9	31	60
Mexico	5	29	44	23
The Netherlands	5	54	31	10
Russia	1	17	57	26
Sweden	6	41	39	14
United Kingdom	2	28	49	21
United States	9	39	35	17

Table 34

AT THIS INSTITUTION, HOW WOULD YOU EVALUATE THE RESEARCH EQUIPMENT AND INSTRUMENTS?

	EXCELLENT	GOOD	FAIR	POOR
Australia	4%	24%	38%	34%
Brazil	2	13	34	51
Chile	1	13	38	48
Germany	10	37	36	18
Hong Kong	8	36	40	16
Israel	1	21	41	38
Japan	2	12	38	48
Korea	1	8	26	65
Mexico	2	20	41	37
The Netherlands	5	53	34	9
Russia	1	6	40	53
Sweden	13	37	35	15
United Kingdom	5	25	41	29
United States	9	32	35	23

Table 35

AT THIS INSTITUTION, HOW WOULD YOU EVALUATE THE COMPUTER FACILITIES?

	EXCELLENT	GOOD	FAIR	POOR
Australia	12%	41%	34%	12%
Brazil	5	21	34	41
Chile	5	28	40	27
Germany	17	43	27	13
Hong Kong	21	49	24	7
Israel	11	45	31	13
Japan	4	21	53	22
Korea	2	11	39	48
Mexico	9	35	39	18
The Netherlands	12	57	23	8
Russia	1	14	38	46
Sweden	22	46	25	7
United Kingdom	8	40	39	13
United States	19	43	28	11

Table 36

AT THIS INSTITUTION, HOW WOULD YOU EVALUATE THE LIBRARY HOLDINGS?

	EXCELLENT	GOOD	FAIR	POOR
Australia	7%	33%	38%	23%
Brazil	8	26	39	27
Chile	4	19	39	38
Germany	12	41	32	15
Hong Kong	8	41	34	17
Israel	6	32	35	27
Japan	7	24	44	24
Korea	1	7	28	65
Mexico	7	32	39	22
The Netherlands	11	54	26	8
Russia	4	35	41	20
Sweden	18	44	26	13
United Kingdom	7	31	39	24
United States	15	35	32	18

Table 37

THIS IS AN ESPECIALLY CREATIVE AND PRODUCTIVE TIME IN MY FIELD.

	AGREE	NEUTRAL	DISAGREE
Australia	67%	21%	12%
Brazil	55	23	22
Chile	62	29	9
Germany	53	30	18
Hong Kong	67	21	13
Israel	63	26	11
Japan	63	29	8
Korea	75	19	6
Mexico	73	17	11
The Netherlands	64	27	9
Russia	51	35	14
Sweden	67	24	9
United Kingdom	63	24	14
United States	71	18	12

Table 38

TO WHAT EXTENT ARE YOU SATISFIED WITH THE COURSES YOU TEACH?

	SATISFIED	NEUTRAL	DISSATISFIED
Australia	77%	16%	7%
Brazil	64	31	5
Chile	78	18	4
Germany	59	27	14
Hong Kong	72	23	5
Israel	81	17	2
Japan	54	35	11
Korea	82	15	3
Mexico	79	16	6
Russia	60	36	4
Sweden	74	21	5
United Kingdom	76	17	7
United States	86	11	4

Table 39

TO WHAT EXTENT ARE YOU SATISFIED WITH THE OPPORTUNITY TO PURSUE YOUR OWN IDEAS?

	SATISFIED	NEUTRAL	DISSATISFIED
Australia	65%	18%	16%
Brazil	45	30	25
Chile	58	21	21
Germany	52	26	23
Hong Kong	57	23	20
Israel	24	38	38
Japan	70	21	10
Korea	26	43	32
Mexico	63	18	19
Russia	29	47	25
Sweden	73	19	9
United Kingdom	67	17	17
United States	77	12	12

Table 40

TO WHAT EXTENT ARE YOU SATISFIED WITH YOUR RELATIONSHIPS WITH COLLEAGUES?

	SATISFIED	NEUTRAL	DISSATISFIED
Australia	69%	21%	10%
Brazil	58	29	13
Chile	69	20	10
Germany	71	20	9
Hong Kong	66	23	11
Israel	74	19	8
Japan	52	38	10
Korea	65	26	10
Mexico	69	21	10
Russia	49	49	2
Sweden	70	22	8
United Kingdom	74	17	9
United States	69	18	13

Table 41

BASED ON YOUR EXPERIENCE AT THIS INSTITUTION, HOW WOULD YOU ASSESS THE INTELLECTUAL ATMOSPHERE?

	EXCELLENT	GOOD	FAIR	POOR
Australia	8%	41%	37%	15%
Brazil	9	51	31	9
Chile	5	34	47	14
Hong Kong	4	37	42	17
Israel	13	46	31	10
Japan	6	26	47	21
Korea	3	20	43	34
Mexico	7	44	37	12
The Netherlands	7	55	32	6
Russia	10	54	33	4
Sweden	10	51	29	10
United States	15	47	30	8

Table 42

THIS IS A POOR TIME FOR ANY YOUNG PERSON TO BEGIN AN ACADEMIC CAREER IN MY FIELD.

	AGREE	NEUTRAL	DISAGREE
Australia	34%	20%	46%
Brazil	48	18	34
Chile	33	25	43
Germany	36	20	44
Hong Kong	23	23	54
Israel	32	15	53
Japan	13	25	62
Korea	20	19	61
Mexico	25	15	60
The Netherlands	29	20	51
Russia	32	26	42
Sweden	18	23	59
United Kingdom	42	21	37
United States	30	16	54

Table 43

IF I HAD IT TO DO OVER AGAIN, I WOULD NOT BECOME AN ACADEMIC.

	AGREE	NEUTRAL	DISAGREE
Australia	16%	18%	66%
Brazil	15	7	78
Chile	16	12	72
Germany	17	15	69
Hong Kong	17	15	69
Israel	9	6	85
Japan	16	30	54
Korea	10	14	76
The Netherlands	13	18	69
Russia	11	17	72
Sweden	8	8	84
United Kingdom	20	17	63
United States	11	10	79

Table 44

HOW INFLUENTIAL ARE YOU, PERSONALLY, IN HELPING TO SHAPE KEY ACADEMIC POLICIES AT THE INSTITUTIONAL LEVEL?

	VERY INFLUENTIAL	SOMEWHAT INFLUENTIAL	A LITTLE INFLUENTIAL	NOT AT ALL INFLUENTIAL
Australia	2%	6%	14%	78%
Brazil	3	18	36	43
Chile	3	14	20	64
Germany	1	5	14	80
Hong Kong	1	6	13	81
Israel	5	7	31	57
Japan	5	24	40	31
Korea	3	8	33	57
Mexico	3	13	23	61
Russia	3	19	25	53
Sweden	5	13	18	64
United Kingdom	2	8	16	74
United States	3	11	22	64

Table 45
BASED ON YOUR EXPERIENCE AT THIS INSTITUTION, HOW WOULD YOU ASSESS RELATIONSHIPS BETWEEN FACULTY AND ADMINISTRATION?

	EXCELLENT	GOOD	FAIR	POOR
Australia	3%	28%	39%	30%
Brazil	6	46	35	12
Chile	3	25	48	24
Hong Kong	3	28	47	22
Israel	9	40	31	20
Japan	3	22	58	18
Korea	1	15	47	38
Mexico	6	43	37	15
The Netherlands	3	29	47	22
Russia	3	47	42	8
Sweden	4	34	41	21
United States	7	36	36	21

Table 46
I AM KEPT INFORMED ABOUT WHAT IS GOING ON AT THIS INSTITUTION.

	AGREE	NEUTRAL	DISAGREE
Australia	36%	22%	42%
Brazil	45	18	37
Chile	35	28	37
Germany	13	20	67
Hong Kong	30	20	50
Israel	31	30	40
Japan	31	34	36
Korea	31	30	39
Mexico	36	21	43
The Netherlands	34	34	33
Russia	45	36	19
Sweden	50	24	26
United Kingdom	31	24	46
United States	43	23	34

Table 47

COMMUNICATION BETWEEN THE FACULTY AND THE ADMINISTRATION IS POOR.

	AGREE	NEUTRAL	DISAGREE
Australia	52%	22%	25%
Brazil	45	18	37
Chile	44	27	28
Germany	62	21	18
Hong Kong	53	23	23
Israel	37	28	34
Japan	43	38	19
Korea	51	27	22
Mexico	54	18	29
The Netherlands	44	32	25
Russia	46	36	19
Sweden	29	40	31
United Kingdom	49	25	26
United States	45	24	32

Table 48

THE ADMINISTRATION IS OFTEN AUTOCRATIC.

	AGREE	NEUTRAL	DISAGREE
Australia	63%	23%	14%
Brazil	44	20	36
Chile	58	23	19
Germany	67	21	13
Hong Kong	64	23	13
Israel	57	24	19
Japan	40	34	26
Korea	46	30	24
Mexico	54	20	27
The Netherlands	37	38	25
Russia	43	41	16
Sweden	43	36	21
United Kingdom	64	21	16
United States	58	22	20

Table 49

LACK OF FACULTY INVOLVEMENT IS A REAL PROBLEM.

	AGREE	NEUTRAL	DISAGREE
Australia	48%	33%	19%
Brazil	60	19	22
Chile	67	18	15
Germany	56	27	17
Hong Kong	54	30	16
Israel	53	25	22
Japan	33	37	30
Korea	45	30	26
Mexico	68	16	17
The Netherlands	40	36	25
Russia	37	48	15
Sweden	25	47	28
United Kingdom	44	34	22
United States	43	28	29

Table 50

TOP-LEVEL ADMINISTRATORS ARE PROVIDING COMPETENT LEADERSHIP.

	AGREE	NEUTRAL	DISAGREE
Australia	29%	26%	46%
Brazil	46	27	27
Chile	28	31	42
Germany	24	27	49
Hong Kong	23	29	48
Israel	28	31	41
Japan	60	22	18
Korea	24	31	45
Mexico	33	23	44
The Netherlands	32	42	26
Russia	30	53	17
Sweden	30	38	32
United Kingdom	26	25	49
United States	39	22	38

Table 51

THE ADMINISTRATION SUPPORTS ACADEMIC FREEDOM.

	AGREE	NEUTRAL	DISAGREE
Australia	44%	33%	24%
Brazil	54	26	20
Chile	48	31	21
Germany	18	26	57
Hong Kong	49	27	24
Israel	72	17	11
Japan	71	23	7
Korea	35	37	28
Mexico	47	22	31
Russia	26	54	21
Sweden	40	37	23
United Kingdom	45	34	21
United States	64	23	14

Table 52

THE GOVERNMENT SHOULD HAVE THE RESPONSIBILITY TO DEFINE THE OVERALL PURPOSES AND POLICIES FOR HIGHER EDUCATION.

	AGREE	NEUTRAL	DISAGREE
Australia	29%	17%	54%
Brazil	45	14	41
Chile	45	24	31
Hong Kong	47	20	33
Israel	32	15	53
Japan	19	33	48
Korea	50	20	30
Mexico	33	16	50
The Netherlands	43	25	32
Russia	90	6	4
Sweden	46	22	33
United States	10	13	77

Table 53

IN THIS COUNTRY, THERE IS FAR TOO MUCH GOVERNMENTAL INTERFERENCE IN IMPORTANT ACADEMIC POLICIES.

	AGREE	NEUTRAL	DISAGREE
Australia	57%	26%	17%
Brazil	42	23	35
Chile	17	32	51
Hong Kong	43	32	25
Israel	31	22	48
Japan	48	41	11
Korea	89	8	3
Mexico	55	22	23
The Netherlands	46	32	22
Russia	33	39	27
Sweden	25	36	39
United States	34	33	33

Table 54

IS ACADEMIC FREEDOM STRONGLY PROTECTED IN THIS COUNTRY?

	YES	NO
Australia	77%	23%
Brazil	38	62
Chile	71	29
Hong Kong	71	30
Israel	92	8
Japan	79	21
Korea	74	26
Mexico	69	31
The Netherlands	74	26
Russia	16	84
Sweden	83	17
United States	81	19

Table 55

I CAN FOCUS MY RESEARCH ON ANY TOPIC OF SPECIAL INTEREST TO ME.

	AGREE	NEUTRAL	DISAGREE
Australia	81%	7%	12%
Brazil	72	12	16
Chile	76	14	11
Germany	63	14	23
Hong Kong	83	8	9
Japan	87	8	5
Korea	85	10	5
Mexico	66	14	20
Russia	65	19	16
Sweden	79	8	13
United Kingdom	79	10	11
United States	89	5	6

Table 56

AT THIS INSTITUTION, I AM FULLY FREE TO DETERMINE THE CONTENT OF THE COURSES I TEACH.

	AGREE	NEUTRAL	DISAGREE
Australia	67%	9%	24%
Brazil	69	9	22
Chile	70	14	17
Germany	61	15	24
Hong Kong	61	9	29
Japan	80	13	7
Korea	90	7	3
Mexico	65	14	21
Russia	45	27	28
Sweden	64	13	24
United Kingdom	62	14	25
United States	78	8	14

Table 57

IN THIS COUNTRY, THERE ARE NO POLITICAL OR IDEOLOGICAL RESTRICTIONS ON WHAT A SCHOLAR MAY PUBLISH.

	AGREE	NEUTRAL	DISAGREE
Australia	59%	21%	20%
Brazil	46	24	31
Chile	75	16	9
Germany	74	11	15
Hong Kong	66	15	19
Israel	79	5	15
Japan	55	26	19
Korea	35	22	43
Mexico	58	16	27
The Netherlands	58	20	23
Russia	40	39	21
Sweden	78	11	12
United Kingdom	55	20	25
United States	49	17	34

Table 58

RESPECT FOR ACADEMICS IS DECLINING.

	AGREE	NEUTRAL	DISAGREE
Australia	57%	32%	11%
Brazil	78	10	12
Chile	51	28	21
Germany	50	29	20
Hong Kong	49	33	18
Israel	60	23	18
Japan	65	30	6
Korea	69	22	9
Mexico	56	20	24
The Netherlands	44	41	15
Russia	64	26	10
Sweden	43	36	21
United Kingdom	73	20	7
United States	64	23	13

Table 59

ACADEMICS ARE AMONG THE MOST INFLUENTIAL OPINION LEADERS IN MY COUNTRY.

	AGREE	NEUTRAL	DISAGREE
Australia	19%	27%	54%
Brazil	39	17	44
Chile	16	30	54
Germany	15	29	56
Hong Kong	26	36	38
Israel	12	26	62
Japan	40	46	15
Korea	63	29	8
Mexico	30	28	42
Russia	24	33	43
Sweden	30	29	41
United Kingdom	11	25	63
United States	21	27	52

Table 60

FACULTY IN MY DISCIPLINE HAVE A PROFESSIONAL OBLIGATION TO APPLY THEIR KNOWLEDGE TO PROBLEMS IN SOCIETY.

	YES	NO
Australia	86%	14%
Brazil	78	22
Chile	74	26
Germany	93	7
Hong Kong	84	16
Israel	76	24
Japan	81	19
Korea	86	14
Mexico	86	14
The Netherlands	87	13
Russia	61	39
Sweden	68	32
United Kingdom	79	21
United States	82	18

Table 61

DURING THE PAST THREE YEARS AT THIS INSTITUTION, HOW FREQUENTLY HAVE FOREIGN STUDENTS BEEN ENROLLED?

	FREQUENTLY	OCCASIONALLY	RARELY	NEVER
Australia	68%	22%	8%	2%
Brazil	25	33	25	17
Chile	34	34	27	6
Hong Kong	13	33	38	16
Israel	27	33	33	7
Japan	58	28	11	3
Korea	0	4	48	47
Mexico	20	33	26	22
Russia	47	11	27	16
Sweden	37	41	17	5
United States	77	19	3	1

Table 62

DURING THE PAST THREE YEARS AT THIS INSTITUTION, HOW FREQUENTLY HAVE YOUR STUDENTS STUDIED ABROAD?

	FREQUENTLY	OCCASIONALLY	RARELY	NEVER
Australia	12%	35%	37%	17%
Brazil	20	35	28	17
Chile	12	31	40	18
Hong Kong	19	40	30	11
Israel	14	29	42	15
Japan	53	28	14	5
Korea	1	11	58	30
Mexico	12	25	31	31
Russia	11	30	45	14
Sweden	25	45	24	7
United States	36	39	19	6

Table 63

THE CURRICULUM AT THIS INSTITUTION SHOULD BE MORE INTERNATIONAL IN FOCUS.

	AGREE	NEUTRAL	DISAGREE
Australia	47%	40%	13%
Brazil	61	22	17
Chile	79	12	9
Germany	57	31	12
Hong Kong	66	27	7
Israel	29	32	39
Japan	67	31	2
Korea	76	20	4
Mexico	75	17	8
Russia	59	39	3
Sweden	59	34	7
United States	45	37	18

Table 64

FOR HOW MANY MONTHS DURING THE PAST THREE YEARS HAVE YOU TRAVELLED ABROAD TO STUDY OR DO RESEARCH?

	ONE OR MORE	NONE
Australia	62%	38%
Brazil	37	63
Chile	61	39
Germany	65	35
Hong Kong	72	28
Israel	93	7
Japan	55	45
Korea	62	38
Mexico	43	57
The Netherlands	70	30
Russia	36	64
Sweden	75	25
United Kingdom	53	47
United States	35	65

Table 65
FOR HOW MANY MONTHS DURING THE PAST THREE YEARS HAVE YOU SERVED AS A FACULTY MEMBER AT AN INSTITUTION IN ANOTHER COUNTRY?

	ONE OR MORE	NONE
Australia	15%	85%
Brazil	6	94
Chile	22	78
Germany	25	75
Hong Kong	30	70
Israel	65	35
Japan	7	93
Korea	7	93
Mexico	12	88
The Netherlands	34	66
Russia	9	91
Sweden	22	78
United Kingdom	16	84
United States	9	91

Table 66
IN ORDER TO KEEP UP WITH DEVELOPMENTS IN MY DISCIPLINE, A SCHOLAR MUST READ BOOKS AND JOURNALS PUBLISHED ABROAD.

	AGREE	NEUTRAL	DISAGREE
Australia	98%	2%	1%
Brazil	92	3	4
Chile	98	1	1
Germany	91	5	4
Hong Kong	98	1	1
Israel	98	2	0
Japan	93	5	2
Korea	96	4	1
Mexico	91	6	3
The Netherlands	95	3	3
Russia	99	1	0
Sweden	96	3	1
United States	62	17	22

Table 67

CONNECTIONS WITH SCHOLARS IN OTHER COUNTRIES ARE VERY IMPORTANT TO MY PROFESSIONAL WORK.

	AGREE	NEUTRAL	DISAGREE
Australia	81%	15%	4%
Brazil	85	11	4
Chile	95	3	2
Germany	78	14	8
Hong Kong	85	12	4
Israel	86	8	6
Japan	88	11	2
Korea	91	8	1
Mexico	79	15	6
The Netherlands	81	11	8
Russia	89	11	1
Sweden	87	11	2
United Kingdom	63	26	11
United States	55	26	19

Table 68

A SCHOLAR'S INTERNATIONAL CONNECTIONS ARE IMPORTANT IN FACULTY EVALUATION AT THIS INSTITUTION.

	AGREE	NEUTRAL	DISAGREE
Australia	58%	28%	14%
Brazil	42	22	36
Chile	62	23	15
Hong Kong	50	32	19
Israel	72	12	16
Japan	65	25	10
Korea	33	24	43
Mexico	54	23	24
Russia	21	39	40
Sweden	64	24	13
United States	32	28	40

Ministry of Education & Training
MET Library